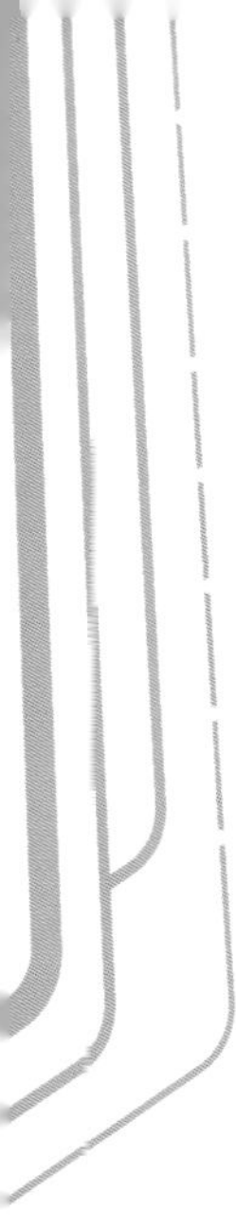

闽南师范大学学术著作出版专项经费资助

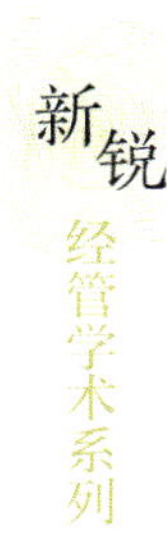
新锐
经管学术系列

金融科技

郝晋辉　著

厦门大学出版社
XIAMEN UNIVERSITY PRESS
国家一级出版社
全国百佳图书出版单位

图书在版编目(CIP)数据

金融科技/郝晋辉著.—厦门:厦门大学出版社,2020.5
(新锐经管学术系列)
ISBN 978-7-5615-5751-8

Ⅰ.①金… Ⅱ.①郝… Ⅲ.①金融—科学技术—研究 Ⅳ.①F830

中国版本图书馆 CIP 数据核字(2020)第 068980 号

出 版 人 郑文礼
责任编辑 江珏玙
封面设计 蒋卓群
技术编辑 许克华

出版发行 厦门大学出版社
社　　址 厦门市软件园二期望海路 39 号
邮政编码 361008
总　　机 0592-2181111 0592-2181406(传真)
营销中心 0592-2184458 0592-2181365
网　　址 http://www.xmupress.com
邮　　箱 xmup@xmupress.com
印　　刷 厦门市金凯龙印刷有限公司

开本 720 mm×1 000 mm 1/16
印张 17.5
插页 2
字数 338 千字
版次 2020 年 5 月第 1 版
印次 2020 年 5 月第 1 次印刷
定价 58.00 元

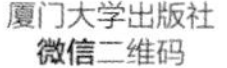

Preface

My first access to the computer was 20 years ago. The rapid development within such a short time in financial technology takes us by a surprise, causing us not to know how to learn it. The reason why it is booming is that three areas such as computer software and hardware, biotechnology, and communicative technology are growing at a fantastic speed, especially in the financial sector ranging from insurance, banking and rent to securities and futures. They are taking the lead in the jaw-dropping growth of the whole industry. The book will discuss what influences it has on the above areas in detail. They can be divided into three main areas ranging from government and traditional finance to technology industry. The book will take these three areas into careful consideration, too. They include financial industry, technology industry and government administrative department. From the deep perspective of implementers and supervisors, financial technology can be segmented into insurance technology and regulatory technology. They are developing slowly in China, compared with that of banking industry.

Risk is opportunities. Against the backdrop of huge demand in the market and bad technology, those who are potential obviously are black horses.

The insurance industry has an extremely important position in the marketization of mainland China. However, various technologies, investment channels, and talents can not keep up with the banking industry. When investing in the stock fund, many large European, American, Japanese, and even Taiwan investors want to take advantage of insurance science and technology, and achieve overtaking on the curve in mainland China earlier.

Government departments around the world, due to the lack of management of digitalization and advanced technology, apparently lag behind, compared with the corporate world. At present, the national leadership of mainland China strongly supports decision-making in blockchain and digital banking. Naturally there is also a great demand for regulatory technology.

This book is composed of four parts: the first is introduction, the second technology, the third application of the financial industry, and the fourth the various cases of financial technology.

The first part: Chapter 1 is to discuss from the history of financial technology(Fintech). What is finance? And what is technology? Analyze from two aspects. Then Chapter 2 comes to how the financial industry has entered the process of science and technology, and how technology companies go into the financial field. Chapter 3 talks about government supervision, which includes the historical development direction and differences of China, the United States, Japan, and Europe.

The second part is the technical article, first the blockchain, and then big data, as well as cloud computing and the internet of things, computer security technology, and artificial intelligence. A good computer or mathematical background is required to understand this part more deeply. If not, just regard it as some basic knowledge.

The third part is the application of the financial industry in commerce, which specifically mentions, banking, the insurance industry, investment and wealth management, credit reporting and other business scene applications.

The fourth part is the actual case, which can be divided into the case of the world and the case of mainland China. The development direction of insurance technology is also specifically discussed.

The rapid development of Fintech is abnormal and cannot be measured. With the maturity of quantum computing, the rapid promotion of 5G communication capabilities, and the sustainable growth of biotechnology, we can feel that the development of the entire financial technology and technology application has unlimited space for imagination.

This book aim to lead students and friends to have a preliminary understanding. If you have any questions, welcome to discuss and enlighten me. Thank you all!

CONTENTS

The First Part

Introduction

Chapter 1 Finance and Technology

1.1 History

In 1946, the world's first electronic computer ENIAC(electronic numerical integrat and computer) was born in the United States. Information technology(IT) was gradually applied in science and other fields. People in the financial industry realized that the ever-changing information technology is the only way to improve the efficiency of the entire financial system, connecting the financial industry with a long history with emerging information technology. Before the application of information technology, the operation of the financial system greatly depends on human labor. With the progress of society, the rapid development of the social economy has generated huge capital flows, and the demand for payment settlement and stock transaction has forced the financial industry to improve the efficiency of background business processing as soon as possible. Since the end of World War Ⅱ, the world has entered a large-scale process of rapid recovery. On the one hand, the quality and circulation of goods have undergone profound changes. On the other hand, the rapid development of science and technology has promoted the improvement of post-war production efficiency, making the scale of national and multinational trade develop rapidly, along with increasing scale of commodity and currency flows.

In 1950, the Stanford Research Institute in the United States demonstrated an electronic accounting system which can read cheque information and process it. ERMA(electronic recording machine-accounting) is designed by Bank of America. Due to the high cost, the problem of information transmission from checks to pierced cards was difficult to solve, so that ERMA has not yet been practically applicable. Nevertheless, ERMA pioneered the use of computers to replace manual check processing. We call it the "financial back-office business electronization" period in which a series of application software was most on improving the background update accounts, accounting systems and printing statements.

In 1970, with the help of electronic computers, communication lines, and disk media, the banking industry's operating efficiency was doubled. Computers mainly play the role of accelerators in banks. The main purpose of banks using computers is to improve the efficiency of bank bookkeeping and reduce operating costs. Commercial banks in the United States not only successively introduced electronic computers, but also developed a series of application software on their own to simulate manual paper and cheque calculations.

In 1980, the process of economic globalization began, the bank business behind the scene became highly electronic, and the financial industry still coundn't meet the ever-growing financial needs. Increasing customer traffic means multiple people queuing, who are just to handle a small amount of small deposits or withdrawals, or to check account balances. Bank staff are tired of the homogeneous needs of a large number of customers, and sometimes inevitably delays, which, to some extent, results in the loss of customers. But through the expansion of branches, the personnel are increased to reduce the number of queuing personnel, and the cost of customers is too high. So bankers began to provide self-service banking services in order to relieve the pressure of banking outlets.

New financial products such as POS (point of sale), electronic funds transfer, electronic wallet smart cards, transactions based on electronic data exchange, and automation have appeared one after another. A major sign of the development of self-service banking services is that major commercial banks have begun to deploy ATMs(automated teller machines) extensively. In the payment field, banks have also begun to try electronically. The existence of huge cash flows needs to be digested. A large amount of social resource is used for the printing of banknotes. The use of electronic storage and circulation and financial front desk business processing has also greatly saved human resources in the financial industry. The need to reduce the number of counter employees in commercial banks is becoming more apparent with the digitization of retail business.

The electronization of financial front desk business has a positive influence on operating cost reduction, and improvement of efficiency and effectiveness of banks. However, due to the efficiency improvement brought about by technological upgrade, the first unemployment epidemic in the banking industry also occurred, angry counter employees of banks even damaged ATMs.

In 1990, Tim Berners Lee invented the Internet, and information technology entered the Internet era. The strong rise of the Internet immediately led to the rapid development of global economy, triggering global business revolution and business revolution, and Internet companies were born one after another.

As the industry introducing the information technology earliest, the financial industry will not miss the Internet, of course. With the rapid development of the Internet technology, the financial institutions with sharp insight begun to actively expand Internet service channels and move standardized financial services to the Internet. The banking industry gradually set up its own online banking. Wells Fargo has started to build online banking since 1992. Now it has the nation's top online service system. In 2013, it became the bank by highest market value in the world, and has won the favor from many investors including Buffett. Supposing ATMs achieving self-service banking services 24/7 span time, then online banking has evolved the convenience of services across space. People can enjoy banking services anytime and anywhere through online banking, such as transfers, remittances, and online payment business.

In 1997, China Merchants Bank launched its website, which lifted the curtain on the development of online banking. The rapid rise of China UnionPay is a classic example of domestic financial electronicization. Under the competitive pressure of strong international payment brands, China UnionPay has basically achieved global goals. At present, the transaction scale of UnionPay cards has reached the third in the world, surpassing international giants such as the US card and the Japanese card.

As the American social predictor John Naisbitt said in his book Megatrends, "The shift from money to electronics is as important as the shift from barter to currency in the past." The first contact between the Internet and finance not only raised the level of financial informatization to an unprecedented level, but also laid a solid foundation for the rapid advancement of financial technology in the 21st century.

In the 21st century, from the first year of Internet finance to Fintech 2.0, the contact between the traditional financial industry and the information technology industry has made world-renowned achievements. The advancement of information technology has enhanced the business processing capabilities of financial institutions, but emerging Internet technology companies should make a foray into the financial industry across borders, which quickly disrupted financial industry.

Case study: Yu'E Bao's success lies in its creative grafting of Internet technology with the long pent-up people's small-amount financial management needs anytime and anywhere, making Internet financial wave in its wake sweep across China. Internet finance mainly refers to the innovation of financial service methods with Internet connection as the main feature under the conditions of the Internet and mobile Internet technology. Therefore, Internet finance is, in essence, financial innovation driven by Internet technology. In recent years, with the rapid advancement of science and technology, emerging technologies such as big data, blockchain, and artificial intelligence have been increasingly applied in various segments of the financial industry, like digital currency, smart credit, Robo-advice, and innovation services. Financial service methods are constantly emerging, the integration of finance and technology is deepening, and Internet finance has entered a new stage. Yu'E Bao's success also heralds the beginning of the Internet's approach to the core of the modern economy—the financial industry.

Throughout the development history of finacial technology (Fintech), it is not difficult to find that the advancement of information technology drives the continuous upgrading and innovation of the financial industry. Not only is the scope of services getting larger and larger, but the service efficiency is getting higher and higher, and the service experience is getting better and better. From a certain point of view, finance and information technology are basically symbiotic, both of whose processing objects are numbers. The connection between the two is inevitable. It is no wonder that Silicon Valley's godfather Jeffrey Muir defines finance in this way: The financial industry is to use computer networks as production equipment to continuously store, process, identify and transmit all the information about the promises and permissions of wealth, and to synchronize wealth with personal life and business activities. We have reason to expect that in the future Fintech will become increasingly closely integrated, and a new era is dawning.

1.2 Evolution

From Fintech 1.0 to 2.0 and from "connection" to "pricing".

The key word of Fintech 1.0 is connection. It only uses the Internet and mobile Internet to connect capital assets and investors to achieve efficient docking on the capital side, to reduce the barrier to entry, and to expand the service population. The link functions of Fintech 1.0 are determined by the characteristics of the Internet.

With the help of the Internet traffic dividend, Fintech 1.0 has expanded customer consumption of financial products from offline to online, and used the Internet as a traffic entrance to aggregate financial services in multiple scenarios on the same platform. Fintech 1.0 improves the docking of the capital side through innovation in business models to improve efficiency. At the Fintech 1.0 stage, technology and finance are more in a relatively simple handover relationship. The role of technology is simply to reinvent financial services as a flow channel or an online product channel for traditional finance.

At the stage 1.0, the relationship between technology and finance are simple grafting, which still belongs to "physical reactions". With the rapid development of emerging technologies such as big data, artificial intelligence, and blockchain, new solutions to the inefficiencies of asset-side pricing have gradually come into being, and Fintech began to enter the stage.

The essence of the stage 2.0 is to integrate advanced technology into the core of financial business, injecting new vitality into traditional finance with a more active attitude. Technological changes such as big data, artificial intelligence and blockchain promote the innovation of asset side and financial infrastructure to be the main propositions of Fintech 2.0.

Typical application scenarios of Fintech 2.0 currently include intelligent supply chain finance, intelligent robot analysis, digital currency, digitization, and cross-border payments.

Fintech 1.0 is an innovation of a business model, while Fintech 2.0 brings a brand-new product design which forms a more accurate matching and pricing on the asset side. The new design of this financial product is not only to connect individuals, but to use the generative fusion of finance and technology to mine portraits of big data from various aspects, digitize asset attributes, then perform efficient and accurate pricing, and finally realize optimized allocation of resources.

The essence of the financial market model is the flow of funds and assets, and the basis of its flow is financial risk pricing. Fintech 2.0 reforms the financial industry, which has provided reasonable risk value levels through technical means and achieved continuous pricing on different assets, thereby achieving efficient and accurate matching of funds and assets. Fintech 2.0 is a radical change in the financial industry, which drives innovation in financial products through information technology, broadens all dimensions of financial services in an orderly manner, and takes a step towards inclusive finance and smart finance.

For example, big data analysis credit reporting services will allow an increasing number of black creditors to remove their dishonest behaviors, so that they can enjoy financial services that match their risks. Intelligent investment driven by artificial intelligence has lowered the threshold for investment and wealth management, making financial services accessible. Blockchain technology, with a subversive gesture, impacts the infrastructure of the financial industry. By means of de-intermediation, it improves market functions and efficiency and completely changes many rules of the traditional financial industry. The innovation of asset side and financial infrastructure driven by technological changes such as big data, artificial intelligence and blockchain is the theme of Fintech 2.0.

1.2.1 Reform of Fintech 2.0

Three driving factors: institution, technology and demand.

1.2.1.1 Institutional reform

Finance, as the core of the modern economy, has always been a supervised-focused industry. Every action of the supervisory institutions has a bearing on the financial industry. China's supervision has always encouraged and supported Fintech. The government has repeatedly encouraged the integration of science and finance and supported conditional financial companies in exploring new technological solutions. The application of financial industry services and an open and inclusive regulatory environment lay a solid foundation for the prosperity of China's financial technology. On the basis of actively encouraging Fintech innovation, the Chinese government has further promoted the construction of market order and the healthy development of the industry through policies and regulations. At the beginning of the development of the Fintech industry, due to the low entry barriers, risk events occurred frequently. Faced with the industry in chaos, the decision-making level strictly guided and regulated financial technology.

In 2016, the Chinese government took encouraging legality and combating illegality as the core principle to promote a one-year Internet financial special overhaul. Therefore, 2016 is also known as the first year of Internet financial supervision.

In 2017, penetrating supervision was fully implemented, and many fields such as enterprises, wealth management, insurance, and funds have officially issued statements, which is conducive to fund regulation in the financial market. With the continuous introduction of various policies, the Fintech industry has developed in the main tone of strict supervision. The once uneven situation has begun to change, and Fintech has returned to normal step by step. Globally, the race between the development of Fintech and the introduction of regulatory policies has become a common phenomenon. Facing the development trend of Fintech, governments of various countries are also actively adjusting their regulatory strategies to find out how to adapt to the development of Fintech in their own countries.

1.2.1.2 Technical reform

Big data is becoming an important means for financial institutions to break through the bottleneck of traditional credit reporting.

As a leaping technology, blockchain is expected to completely subvert the existing inter-agency credit transfer model. The core business of the entire financial industry and the matching of risks and returns may be completed in an unforeseen way on a platform supported by strong technology.

The market has been paying attention to big data analysis technology for some time. As the online behavior of users is getting more and more frequent, the application fields of big data analysis are becoming wider and wider, such as in advertising marketing, credit reporting and risk control. After years of data accumulation, the magnitude of big data, the analysis speed, and the types of data have changed rapidly.

The rise of smart hardware, such as wearable devices and smart homes, has once again expanded the dimension of data, making available data dimensions expand offline. Big data can solve the problem of collecting and storing huge amounts of credit information. On this basis, it can extract the correlation among a large number of data fragments, extract valuable credit information, providing richer raw materials for credit scoring. Supported by emerging technologies, the data scale is getting larger and larger, the data dimension is getting wider and wider, and the model is continuously improved. Big data is becoming an important means for financial institutions to break through the bottleneck of traditional credit reporting.

Blockchain, as the basic technology of Bitcoin, did not attract much attention at the early stage of development. However, as the decentralization, high security and immutability of blockchain was gradually recognized by everyone, financial institutions have gradually started to accept blockchain.

In 2016, Barclays Bank of the United Kingdom completed the world's first trade using blockchain technology for settlement. The settlement took less than 4 hours, much faster than the usual 7—10 days. We can say that the blockchain technology has an edge. At the same time, a number of alliances of blockchain technology have emerged and their development has been quite obvious. IBM's global head of financial markets in London said that for blockchain, 2016 was "a year in which concept is verified, and 2017 was a year in which action is taken".

1.2.1.3 Explosive demand

As China's economy enters a new normal, domestic personal wealth has grown steadily. The Boston Consulting Group reports that as of the end of 2015, China's total personal investable financial assets were about 113 trillion yuan. The total investment financial assets will reach nearly 200 trillion yuan, with a compound annual growth rate of about 12%, far exceeding the world's 5.9% growth until the end of 2020. The accumulation of social wealth and the change in people's traditional concept of focusing on saving over investing have effectively stimulated the overall demand for financial services in the society. However, facing increasing financial demands, the supply of financial services by traditional financial institutions is insufficient. For example, the long-tail financial needs of individuals with a low and medium net worth and small and micro enterprises have never been effectively met.

From the perspective of the financial needs of enterprises, the number of small and micro enterprises is huge, contributing greatly to China's economic development. They, however, have low support in traditional financial institutions.

According to the latest data, the number of China's small and micro enterprises now are close to 90% of the total number of Chinese enterprises, contributing over 60% to GDP (gross domestic product). Their contribution to taxation has exceeded 50%, providing nearly 70% of the import and export trade volume, which has created 80% of urban jobs, contributed 65% to inventions, and 80% to technology. However, more than 55% of the financial credit needs of small and micro enterprises have not been effectively supported. According to estimates, the financing gap for small and micro enterprises is about 2 trillion yuan. In addition to financing services, transfer settlement, tax payment on behalf of enterprises, annual review of licenses, wages issuance on behalf of employers, and cash flow management are also financial services in which small and micro enterprises in China are in great demand.

The same is true for the wealth management market. As wealth management services consume a lot of time and energy of wealth managers, traditional private bank wealth management services are costly.

Due to high operating costs, the threshold for traditional private bank wealth management is mostly 1 million yuan. Some private banks even set the threshold at 10 million yuan, mainly for customers with high net worth. It is difficult for ordinary residents to enjoy professional financial services. On the other hand, traditional financial institutions' risk control methods are relatively simple, unable to price risk for these long-tail users, thereby failing to provide financial services that match their risks. Due to the irregular financial status of the long-tail population, the strong characteristics that the traditional financial institutions' risk control system relies on are lacking, such as credit reporting history, bank flow, work certification, and social security. Besides, it is difficult for traditional risk control systems to collect some weak characteristics of borrowers related to credit, such as credit status, reputation, living habits, and social interaction. The asymmetry of information directly causes that financial institutions have difficulty in price risk for this part of the population. Small and micro enterprises are also troubled by this as individuals. At present, the complete information data of small and micro enterprises in China mainly comes from multiple government departments such as industry and commerce, taxation, customs, finance, quality inspection, labor security, and many non-governmental departments such as banking and telecommunications. These departments have their independent management systems and information confidentiality mechanisms, and the information standards between them are different. There is no information sharing platform, which makes the small and micro enterprises' credit information and data inconvenient to flow and to be disclosed. The openness degree and sharing utilization is low, increasing the difficulty in obtaining information for credit evaluators and information users, and affecting traditional financial institutions' accurate risk pricing on small and micro enterprises. The lack of services of traditional financial institutions has contributed to the failure of a large number of long-tail needs to be met, which is conducive to the rise of Fintech.

At present, the growth rate of Internet financial users far exceeds that of Internet users. Among them, payment and wealth management and stock trading users are typical representatives of Internet users. Online financial consumption is gradually being developed and has become another demand bonus for Fintech.

With the development of the real economy, the functions of financial services are constantly expanding, and the focus of services is also changing. Since the reform and opening-up, China's economic development has ushered in the era of trade, factories, resources, and new economy. At the beginning of reform and opening up, with the loosening of the planned economic system, people's demand for commodities began to recover. The circulation of commodities began to accelerate, and the era of the Chinese economy represented by import and export trade was dawning. At this point, small merchants walking the streets have made a financial service corresponding to the era mark, which is private lending based on acquaintance relationships. The typical example is Wenzhou's developed private lending, which played a crucial role at the early stage of Wenzhou's economic development.

With the continuous improvement of China's productivity and the acceleration of reform and opening-up, relying on the population base of China, low labor costs, and excellent quality of the Chinese people, China soon became a "world factory". At the same time, the Chinese economy officially entered the era of factories represented by industrial production and "Made in China" began to sweep the seven seas with an irresistible trend. During this period, the banking system met the urgent need for financing flow of many factories, and made great contributions to the rapid development of the real economy at that time. With further development of China's industrial economy, huge resource demands are placed before the entire society. The vast number of factories need strong resource systems for support, and China's resource-based enterprises have ushered in a period of rapid development, such as steel production enterprises, coal production enterprises and mineral oil production enterprises. At the same time, after the people's basic needs for clothes and food were met, the rank and file been to pursue better transporting and housing conditions. Automobile manufacturers and real estate development companies began to grow and develop in this period, and the Chinese economy begun to enter the era of resources represented by the real estate industry in which the capital market provided lower-cost and more convenient channels for direct financing of leading enterprises, which is a driving force for the rapid development of enterprises in this period.

Since the 21st century, the Internet and mobile Internet have ushered in a new era. In the era of the new economy, various new business models have emerged. Business models featuring light assets, big data, and the sharing economy have upended the traditional business models of the real economy. As the new economy sweeps across the globe, constrained by factors such as information asymmetry, security issues, and time and space, traditional finance faces many insurmountable obstacles in serving the new economy. The new economy enterprises no longer have the same huge fixed assets as before, which cannot be mortgaged to banks to obtain loans, and even without profits as a result of long-term losses. According to the bank's traditional risk control methods, it is impossible to lend to such enterprises. For individuals, the vast group has no historical record in the bank, and there is no real estate under their name that can be used as collateral, making them fail to get financial support from the bank. In recent years, the advent of Fintech has brought us the dawn of new finance. Fintech applies the latest mobile internet, big data, cloud computing, and blockchain technology like a hot cake to the financial field, which can effectively make up for the shortcomings of traditional finance such as information asymmetry, security issues, and constraints in space and time. The financial needs of enterprises and individuals in the new economy era mentioned above are well addressed by technical means. The new economy era calls for financial technology, whose development, in turn, lay a solid foundation for the dawn of the new economy era.

1.3 Future

1.3.1 Future of Fintech

It will be divided into three stages including development, integration, and formation

The key word at the first stage is development, that is, the further development of emerging Fintech 2.0 is mature and applied, and efficiency of a large number of emerging financial industries has been improved.

The key word at the second stage is integration, that is, technology integrates to produce a large number of new formats, new methods, and new players that have not been seen before. We call them new financial species.

The key word at the third stage is formation. By then, a new value of financial infrastructure will be formed. A large number of applications and the Internet will be basically completed. Today well-recognized financial institutions with a huge number of personnel and financial branches all over the world will disappear.

1.3.1.1 Development

Technology has gradually been cutting-edge, and large-scale applications have emerged. The rise of Fintech 2.0 is characterized by emerging technologies such as big data, blockchain, and artificial intelligence, and their development and evolution are further deepening the origin of finance, improving the underlying infrastructure of finance, and achieving accurate high pricing on the asset side. At present, Fintech 2.0 is still at a relatively immature stage. Big data management and artificial intelligence have not yet been mature from a technical perspective. The maturity of technology is the prerequisite for the outbreak of application. Although these representative technologies of Fintech 2.0 are not yet fully mature, their rapid development is unstoppable. Artificial intelligence has always been at the forefront of technological exploration. Driven by deep learning in recent years, the field is developing explosively. Many technology giants, such as Google, Facebook, IBM, Amazon, and domestic companies such as Baidu and Tencent, have invested a lot of resources to make in-depth layouts in various fields of artificial intelligence. In the financial field, smart credit, smart investment and other directions, financial technology has also become popular. Due to high funding and technical threshold for the development and implementation of artificial intelligence, the current application of artificial intelligence in the financial industry is still limited in attempts in some sub-fields.

Financial institutions have adopted a large number of emerging technologies. With the improvement of financial services efficiency and cost reduction brought about by new technologies, the financial threshold will continue to decrease. Over time, everyone will enjoy financial services matching with their own risk repayment ability in the future, and inclusive finance will be realized. Financial regulators will adopt a large number of emerging technologies. Through big data and artificial intelligence technology, it is possible to monitor changes in financial markets in real time, predict risks, and respond in a timely manner.

1.3.1.2 Integration

At the integration stage, the huge advancement that Fintech brought to the financial industry is, in essence, a solution to the problems that have long restricted the operating efficiency of the financial industry from the technical perspective. Credit is the core element supporting this flow, while its other side is risk.

The risk comes from the middle channel, the ultimate borrower, and various unknowns, so we have to think about it. The balance between risk and efficiency is the eternal theme of the financial industry. Therefore, through the intervention of new technologies, the problems of future financial industry will be solved in the way of internal transformation and upgrading.

With the impact of Fintech companies, traditional financial institutions continue to develop in tune with the changing times, but their actions are slow, and whatever cannot keep up with the changes will eventually be eliminated by the times.

The most significant change was the growing dominance of technology companies. They met the requirements of people for information, sharing and communication by fast-spread, more interactive, and timely Internet. From news portals, or even earlier electronic bulletin boards age, Internet-based information reporting had had delivered a heavy blow to traditional paper media. In its wake, online audio and video rose. The Internet began to "invade" the territory of traditional radio and television. With the advent of Web 2.0 (the second generation of the Internet) and the rise of social networks, the outreach of media has also changed dramatically. As a new form of media, we-media has gradually become an important way for people to obtain information. The low tide of traditional media is not determined by someone, but the inevitable result of the development of information communication technology and the enlargement of the demand for information acquisition.

Another significant change was the start of the decentralization process. Traditional media is elite. Newspapers, magazines, radio, and television are responsible for communicating content, and opinions.

They even have an obligation to education. Ordinary individuals have no means or ability to make sounds. Since mankind entered the information age, the cost of sending out voices has been greatly reduced, and the decentralization process of information spread is inevitably continuing. Regardless of the timeliness or effectiveness of information transmission, the Internet world (compared with the physical world) has become the main power. Whether just individuals or official social media platforms, social media platforms have also become standard in government, enterprises and institutions. In an era where everyone can speak, the decentralization of the media has become an irreversible trend.

It is not difficult to imagine that in the future, the change of Fintech to traditional financial institutions will undergo a similar process: one is the inevitable rise of emerging Fintech companies, and the other is the decentralization of the financial industry. These two processes occur simultaneously. Traditional financial institutions will also adopt new technologies in the process of new financial market competition, and business changes will also occur. Those who are self-styled will soon become the fossils of the previous era; those who embrace change will be reborn and transformed into Fintech companies of the next era.

There is also an important change: with the completion of the digitization of currency, equity, debt and other types of assets, their flow and transaction efficiency will be unprecedentedly improved. Even in the future, people can use funds, securities, and bonds to make direct payment. They will function as currency, and a variety of new transaction forms will be generated one after another. Therefore, in the future, the characteristics and business differentiation of various types of financial services will not be as clear-cut as those in today's banking, securities, insurance, and third-party payments. Platform-based Fintech companies may emerge, covering various existing financial businesses and forms of finance, and developing new financial formats.

A large number of smart devices will become the subject of finance just like people. Smart devices will increasingly reach people's "money bags", and more value exchange will occur directly between things. We can imagine that domestic smart appliances can automatically sign a small loan contract with the power supplier when the electricity bill is about to run out to prevent power failure because of forgetting to pay the electricity bill; the car that is about to arrive in the garage signs a credit guarantee lease with the garage that there will be reserved space after entering the garage, and the integration of financial technology and the internet of things will greatly expand the boundaries of finance. We will usher in an era where the boundaries between finance and the economy are gradually blurring and even disappearing, and we will also usher in an era from finance for all to finance for everything.

1.3.1.3 Formation

A new financial infrastructure is formed, and the substitution of machines to humans is basically complete.

Financial infrastructure refers to the hardware facilities and institutional arrangements for financial operations. The financial activities of the era must run on the corresponding financial infrastructure. In the change of human society, we see that the upgrading of financial infrastructure has improved efficiency of financial activity. In the agricultural society, financial activities between people must manifest themselves as loans between acquaintances. After the industrial revolution, with the development of the commodity economy, credit intermediaries such as banks appeared, and financial activities could be conducted more among strangers. This led to a set of legal and regulatory systems, and eventually formed bank-centered financial infrastructure in the industrial age. Up to now, although our financial infrastructure has absorbed a large amount of Internet technology at the technical level, it is still the system established after the Industrial Revolution structurally and essentially. With the rapid expansion of the world's economic volume and the rapid development of the scientific and technological revolution, the weakness of the original financial infrastructure has become increasingly prominent. The efficiency of financial intermediaries and their ability to predict financial risks are not satisfactory. The financial "tsunami" of 2008 seems far away, but the financial crisis has never ended. Now, emerging technologies such as cloud computing, big data, blockchain, and artificial intelligence are impacting and replacing the old financial infrastructure at an unprecedented speed. The core of financial infrastructure will gradually evolve from structural and institutional design issues to technology problem.

On the Internet of Value, a large number of financial applications will complete various financial services with asset risk pricing as the core, fully realize the financial intelligence, and machine will replace human in the financial industry. The financial system of this era is very different from that in the past. The most important feature is that the core role of participating in the financial industry is no longer a financial institution or a technology company, but a large number of financial applications constructed by artificial intelligence technology. Building a core technology for a new financial infrastructure is the integration of key technologies included in current Fintech 2.0, which can be simply expressed as "CBA": C is cloud computing, B represents big data and blockchain, and A is artificial intelligence (AI). The lowest level is cloud computing. With the deep development of the digital age, cloud computing is not only the financial infrastructure, but also the bottom of the entire digital society. In fact, cloud computing itself is not directly related to finance, but provides the most basic underlying operating platform for finance. Above cloud computing are big data and blockchain. First of all, blockchain is the core technology for building the Internet of Value, which will guarantee the flow of various types of digital assets; at the same time, blockchain will also help us solve the problem of no data owner in the era of big data, data sharing, and right confirmation, creating the basis for the reliable and large-scale application of the big data. With the support of big data and blockchain technology, data usage regulations will change dramatically, and utilization efficiency will be greatly improved. Based on this, artificial intelligence will further develop, and finally digitization and intelligence of finance will be realized.

Financial applications have begun to play a central role in the financial industry. On the Internet of Value, data can flow securely, assets can circulate efficiently, contracts can be executed automatically, and pricing can be done intelligently, which has prompted financial applications developed based on the Internet of Value to fully realize functions of finance. Financial applications will comprehensively replace the once-huge financial institution branches and various sectors. Value transfer is the core element of financial activities. Fintech will make the advancement of human beings possible. The disruption of Fintech to society is not another Internet, but a dramatic change caused by the interconnection of information and value.

Chapter 2 Development of Financial Technology

2.1 Chinese financial technology enterprise is pursuing development

China is becoming the world's largest financial technology market. The ever-increasing financial investment has made China overtake developed countries in entering digital financial era, which has been recognized by several international research institutions. As a result, China has secured a place in financial technology market. Meanwhile, China is taking over ever shrinking western market, making it the regions that most attract eyeballs from financial technology investors across the globe. Ant Financial has ranked the number one now in the world. Four companies including Shanghai Lujiazui International Financial Asset Exchange Co.,Ltd. and Jingdong Financial are among the top ten on the list.

2.1.1 The Internet and mobile payment

The third-party payment belongs to e-commerce industry based on the development of China's earliest, largest and maturest segmentation market. China, with the mobile payment on large scale and still rising, is the largest country applying mobile payment, which calls for more vigorous and stronger regulation and improved systems. China has a vast number of mobile payment users, and the annual overall transaction scale of the Internet payment industry is increasing. In the meanwhile, supervision on the Internet and mobile payment is becoming stronger. Administrative Measures for Payment Services of Non-Financial Institutions in 2010 has included the third-party payment institutions in regulation. Since 2015, the managers have had stronger regulation. As a result, Administrative Measures for Online Payment Business of Non-Bank Payment Institution's pricing mechanism for bank card swipe fee, and QR code payment business specifications, have been introduced subsequently.

A number of online and mobile payment platforms are leading the world, especially Alipay and Tencent, which account for the high financial market, thereby monopolizing the market. Alipay pioneers the guarantee transaction model, which focuses on the development of online service advantages. We Chat is based on the frequency of social interaction and develops fund payment. Other small-scale payment institutions vary.

Case study: Alipay and We Chat competed for red packets in an attempt to promote their own payment system. Tencent, the owner of We Chat, recommends that 400 million We Chat users send virtual red packets to each other. After receiving them, the money will go to mobile payment accounts automatically, which ensures WeChat great success. Users sent 40 million virtual red packets each other, and had mobile payment records with a total worth of 400 million yuan. Jack Ma called it Pearl Harbor Attack on Alipay. Alipay responded immediately by introducing red-packet functions. After that, We Chat announced that it would give 800 million yuan to customers who use virtual red packets as a lush present, and curtail interaction between Alipay users and We Chat users. Finally, We Chat, under the control of Tencent, won the battle. Also, the number of We Chat connected to your bank accounts has increased dramatically.

2.1.2 Online financing

Other countries lag far behind China in the scale of online financing market. Online financing can fall into two categories, and both of them are developing fast.

The first is P2P. P2P has risen by nearly 4.55 times in the number since March 2012, with a cumulative transaction value of 3.3 trillion yuan, of which transaction value in 2012 is about 2 trillion yuan. The P2P' average investment interest rates are 14.96%, 10.83% and 9.93% respectively, which are falling annually. One reason is that market interest rates have been kept in a relatively low level in recent years. The other cause is that there is an explosion in transaction platforms, providing more sufficient fund. P2P plays an important role in our traditional fund lending market. There is something wrong with the platforms due to social credit system, as well as asymmetrical information between platforms and constraint system on creditors. In order to solve this problem, China has raised uniform standards in market access, fund monitoring and internal-control management, which is bound to have an impact on the overall business scale and customer numbers. It pays companies that have formal industries to remove agencies in violation of laws and regulations by dealing with the chaotic phenomena of P2P. There is still room for improvement for P2P platforms in China considering China's large population and their strong demand for financing. In the future, we will make breakthroughs in the technology field such as big data, thus achieving greater development.

The second is crowd funding. China is still in its infancy in this field. Crowd funding platforms are mainly divided into two parts. One is integrated platforms that are related to multiple fields, such as Jingdong Crowd Funding and Taobao Crowd Funding. The other is emerging professional vertical crowd funding platforms that focus on agriculture, movie and entertainment, and automobile and real estate, which is the mainstream of the development of crowd funding.

P2P is on track of fast development. Creditease (act as an catalyst for the internationalization of the industry), PPDF (belong to the first batch of online lending platforms), Shenzhen Hongling Venture Capital Investment Co., Ltd., and Renrendai (the first batch of large-scale platforms) can represent the industry. Eight companies such as Jingdong Crowd Funding and Taobao Crowd Funding secure the top 8 places. Most of them are equity-typed, following right-and-interest type and integrated type. PPDF represents China's first batch of online lending platforms. Later a number of large-scale and influential online lending platforms such as Shenzhen Hongling Venture Capital Investment Co., Ltd., and Renrendai emerged in China. The industry is on track of fast development thanks to these financial technology companies. In terms of crowd funding, Beijing Human Creation Consultation Co., Ltd. issued a report, which rates domestic crowd funding platforms for the first time. Fifty good platforms were selected from over 400 crowd funding platforms and they were classified into four levels. Eight platforms such as Jingdong Crowd Funding, Taobao Crowd Funding, Suning Crowd Funding, Jingdong Dongjia, Zhongbangchou, and Crowd Funding Internet top the crowdfunding industry with A+ level, according to the report.

Case study: About P2P. PPDF reached 200 trillion yuan on transaction amounts last year, and extended to the middle and western of China. The platform reached 198.78 trillion yuan of transaction amounts in 2016, serving 3.38 million debtors, the number of which accounted for 38.58% of the industry's debtors, and prompting 7.11 million lending, 98% of which was within 10,000 yuan. Henan, Sichuan, Hubei and other regions in the middle and western China ranked first in transaction amounts in every province. The development of lending online finance, in turn, is bridging the gap between regions.

On the crowd funding side, Haier Nen oven T3 crowd funding during the first week set a record for Jingdong Crowd Funding platform. Since 2015, intelligent hardware has developed rapidly. In this context, Haier Nen Oven T3 from Xiaobei Technology Avenue, a subsidiary of Haier Group, went online on JD.com on October 25, 2016. On the first day, it reached the crowd funding goal of 500,000 yuan, creating Jingdong Crowd Funding and smart kitchen electricity full-time records.

2.1.3 Smart financial wealth management services

Domestic smart financial wealth management services have developed rapidly in recent years. Each platform generally focuses on certain types of markets based on its own advantages, such as quantitative investment in fixed income to seek differentiated development. However, due to policy and regulatory constraints, each platform can only achieve a general direction about asset planning and product recommendation, which can not yet achieve true intelligent wealth management. Domestic smart financial wealth management services are still in its infancy, and there is a gap compared with foreign advanced platforms. There are currently three factors hindering the development of smart investment in China. First, investors are not mature enough. Second, there are restrictions on investment directions. Third, supervision is relatively vague. At present, the regulatory authorities have a vague attitude towards digital asset allocation business. Though not called P2P, many platforms under the banner of smart investment technology and finance cannot evade supervision and rectification. They can be divided into three types. The first type is the advisory type. Such platforms provide investment advice. The second one is based on asset allocation. These platforms use stock and bond ETFs(exchange traded funds) as investment targets and accept partial or full entrustment by customers. The third one is an asset management type, which can manage assets for customers. The market for intelligent financial wealth management services has huge potential, and robotic wealth management consultants will become the mainstream in the next three to five years in the market. Financial consumers need to gradually accept this model. Financial markets and products are relatively complicated. Whether intelligent machines can achieve self-learning, improve themselves and provide personalized investment advice that is better than existing financial institutions and professional financial managers, remains to be tested by the market. It is far from mature, and a big impact on the existing wealth management model.

Financial companies are a solid force in providing intelligent investment advisory services in China. Some companies have launched their own intelligent investment advisory platforms to provide consumers with financial services, such as JD.com, Jucai plus, and Yitou. They use transaction algorithms to match investors' risk appetites and investment goals, and provide Chinese merchants with low-cost, internationalized management services.

Case study: JD.com builds a personal asset housekeeper at your fingertips. In August 2016, JD Finance launched a brand-new asset stewardship function and smart investment products. The intelligent housekeeper is based on the results of the user's risk tolerance assessment. The intelligent investment system conducts detailed financial ana lysis to recommend practical and effective investment recommendations with a wide range to customers.

2.1.4 Blockchain technology

The subversive nature of the blockchain technology have made domestic technology companies pay close attention to blockchain technology data, and technology giants such as Alibaba and Tencent have started a business quite large in numbers. Technology companies have also joined the ranks of the research and development army.

Case study: Alipay's first blockchain charity project came out. At present, the Alipay Love Donation Platform under Ant Financial Services announced the full introduction of blockchain technology and opened it to public welfare organizations. After review, the signatory organizations can self-publish the public welfare projects on the blockchain. The blockchain technology can be used as an unchangeable digital account book technology, which can minimize human errors, and provide great convenience for data statistics and project execution tracking of public welfare organizations. The flow of funds on third-party platforms allows public welfare projects to be recognized by more public.

2.2 Transformation of traditional financial institutions

On the overall side, traditional financial institutions are another obstacle to the development of Fintech in China. Focused on funds and risks, they have formed a sacred culture for a long time. Business culture started late in some aspects of economic Fintech, and its sensitivity to the market lags behind technology companies. At the same time, the experience provided by traditional financial institutions to customers in certain fields is not as good as that of Fintech companies, which has also swayed customers' choices. However, banks are highly standardized, have a large customer base, and have strong risk control capabilities. They still have great potential to embrace Fintech in the future.

2.2.1 The Internet and mobile payment

Traditional financial institutions in this area are currently facing big challenges. Non-bank payment institutions attract a large number of retail users to turn their payment way from cash to mobile payments, which challenges the traditional bank card fees. According to estimates, banks have lost $152 billion in bank card fees due to the Internet and mobile payments. In order to reverse the trend, banks have adopted two approaches at present. First, Apple, Samsung, and the banking industry sent representatives to grab the payment field. The second is the launch of code-scanning payment systems, such as China Construction Bank Dragon Payment, which currently supports two-dimensional code scanning and payment, focusing on the third- and fourth-tier cities. China Construction Bank's mobile payment cloud flash payment leads the era of cardless payment.

Case study: Industrial and Commercial Bank of China welcomes financial technology in an all-round way, carries out innovations around Internet finance, blockchain, biometrics, quantum communication and other technologies, and strives to enhance its innovative development capabilities.

China Construction Bank has been cooperating with China UnionPay since September 2011 to withdraw from the cash payment model, and has begun to continuously explore and develop mobile payment products. It withdrew from the SIM card model based on mobile package, and developed all-phone model products and launched the Longka cloud flash. Its features are as follows. First, it's simple and convenient to apply for and does not require signing a contract. Second, it supports debits and credits. Third, it supports bank card charge. Based on the above, it is more convenient.

2.2.2 Internet financing

There already being relatively mature business models, traditional financial institutions, such as banks that do not directly access online financing, mainly participate in the form of cooperation between subsidiaries and technology companies. The first is the establishment of P2P subsidiaries. China Development Bank, Ping An Group and other traditional financial institutions have already had good practices. The second is to cooperate with P2P companies. On the crowdfunding side, they not only launch crowdfunding financial products, such as Sunshine Insurance, and crowdfunding insurance products, but also introduce a crowdfunding platform such as the movie Lost in Hong Kong, which is in cooperation with the credit card center of SPDB(SPD Bank). The retail transaction volume in the first three quarters of 2016 in Lufax exceeded 1 trillion yuan.

Case study: Lufax's retail transaction volume in the first three quarters of 2016 exceeded 1 trillion yuan. As of September 30, 2016, the number of registered users on the Lufax platform was 25.5 million, an increase of 39.3% from the beginning of 2016. The number of active users was 6.55 million, an increase of 80.4% from the beginning of the year, continuing to lead the industry. Lufax also has had a number of initiatives in Internet financial innovation, and successfully launched the KYC 2.0 system. Accurate matching is achieved so that the right people can buy the right investment products, thus protecting the interests of investors through the system.

Classic case of crowfunding insurance: It's about Sun Insurance Aishengji. Aishengji is a new type of insurance product launched by Sunshine Insurance, which is regarded as the representative of Internet insurance and is a subversive insurance product. The rules are as follows: First, users can purchase one-year children critical illness insurance, which is only limited to parents' purchase for their children and is only sold on Sunshine Insurance's We Chat public account. When the insurance limit is upgraded, purchasers can increase the coverage by sharing the purchase link. Second, position it as a brand-new mutual help insurance in which people care each other given the concept of participation, which benefits all participants.

2.2.3 Robo Adviser

Robo Adviser has been put under spotlight in the wealth management market. Following the frequent entry of online financial institutions, traditional banks have begun to deploy the field of intelligent investment consulting. The main intervention method is to develop investment consulting apps, and provide customers with robot consultancy services. In fact, traditional financial institutions have certain inherent advantages when they are involved in intelligent investment consulting, such as strong R & D strength, advanced risk control technology and customer service experience. The reason why traditional financial institutions have a better foundation for developing intelligent investment consulting products is that they have high customer trust.

Consumers in China often believe that the bank will not go bankrupt without losing money. Therefore, banks' involvement in intelligent investment consulting can gather a large number of users in a short time. This, however, also poses a challenge to banks. If customers trust the banks blindly, they will complain to the bank when the product loses, which may trigger social disharmony.

Case study: China Merchants Bank launched Capricorn Investment to test the smart investment consulting industry, which uses machine learning algorithms and incorporates more than a decade of experience of China Merchants Bank to build a "smart fund portfolio allocation service" based on cemetery funds and global asset allocation.

2.2.4 Blockchain technology

The blockchain technology can establish a service model which subverts the traditional financial credit center by decentralizing from the technical level. At present, financial institutions focus on the blockchain technology. The application of the blockchain technology in the financial industry includes three aspects. The first is the application of Over-The-Counter transactions, including the fields of global payment remittance and securities transaction network lending. The second is the application of rights confirmation, including the fields of securities registration and asset mortgage. The third is the application of registration, including records of customer information and transaction information. Judging from the practice of domestic financial institutions, emerging network banks on the stock exchange have carried out forward-looking research and active practice on the blockchain technology due to the urgent need for fund reconciliation. This technology has the characteristics of high efficiency, security, availability, and expansibility. The tedious problems of inter-bank data exchange, clearing and posting are well solved, and the smooth progress of inter-bank cooperative loan business is guaranteed.

Case study: Weizhong Bank's blockchain practice from real-time clearing systems to cloud service platforms. Weizhong Bank and Huarui Bank developed an inter-bank joint loan clearing platform based on the alliance-type blockchain technology and launched it for trial operation to optimize the settlement and clearing of the "microparticle loan" joint loan of the two banks, an online personal microcredit loan product of Weizhong Bank, which adopts the inter-bank cooperation model.

Through this platform, Weizhong Bank and the cooperative banks have jointly stored and maintained loan reserve account information, which is non-temperable, traceable, and relatively secure. At the same time, the previously required reconciliation cycle has been reduced to real-time, and the cooperative bank can understand the changes in the bank's reserve fund account and fund transaction information in real time to improve settlement efficiency without the need for additional system development.

2.3 Conclusion

(1) China's Fintech market is large in scale and has many technical and comprehensive advantages: when it comes to the data and indicators, especially in terms of payment and online financing, China is indeed leading in some of the Fintech subdivisions. The catch-up is more due to China's huge population base and market size. However, from the perspective of the development potential of the industry, our advantage is still relatively low in the global ranking. From the perspective of technological development, the financial foundation, especially financial infrastructure construction, is the core factor supporting Fintech innovation and international competitiveness. We still lag behind foreign countries in this respect.

(2) Fintech has shifted its model from "filling the gap" to starting to impact the entire traditional finance. First, from the perspective of development drivers, Chinese-style filling of the gap will gradually transition to American-typed better service. Due to the size of the Chinese market, even the filling has made China's Fintech share bigger and development much faster than the United States. In the United States, the motivation for the development of the Fintech industry is more in

the original intention of providing better services because the financial system is relatively mature. Second, from the perspective of new and old financial cooperation, Fintech and large-scale traditional financial cooperation have been involved in the entire traditional financial model. The entire process from customer acquisition to risk management and control is changing. This trend is clearer, especially in the United States.

(3) Fintech has turned from domestic exploration to internationalization. From the perspective of the cross-border exhibition industry model, the Internet and mobile payment are the most concentrated areas, and the payment giants have stronger strategies and capabilities than abroad. The foreign investment access policy for payments and other businesses is closely related. From the perspective of subdivided fields, in addition to payments, it is entirely possible for the future elec tronic money such as crowdfunding network financing to turn from a sporadic cross-border operation to comprehensive globalization.

2.4 Current situations of development of financial technology abroad

2.4.1 America

In the process of promoting the development of financial technology, the United States has gradually formed a relatively scientific financing model, improved legal system, and more complete supporting measures.

2.4.1.1 Risk leasing

Risk leasing is an emerging financing method for startups. In this model, risk leasing companies reach an agreement with startups to invest in and purchase technology and equipment they need and lease them to these firms. They pay monthly fees, including rents, taxes and maintenance fees. When the lease agreement is about to expire, startups can choose to buy the equipment with assets or warrants based on their own profitability. Risk leasing is one of the earliest forms of risk loans. In the 1970s, with the development of risk leasing and start-up investment institutions, some banks in the northeastern United States began to consider risk loans, including from First National Bank of Boston and Bank of New England, which believed that the involvement of start-up investment institutions can reduce the risk of bankruptcy and collapse of startups. Under the circumstance that startup investment institutions simultaneously own equity, patents and intellectual property rights of startups, they have extra sources of repayment, with reduced risks of repayment. Therefore, those banks in the northeast of the United States began to establish long-term partnerships with start-up investment institutions. By investigating and researching start-ups before lending, start-up investment institutions made risk loans to companies based on their own assessments at the early stages of business startups. The operation mode of risk loans is similar to that of risk leasing, but banks will set thresholds for items such as liquidity, net asset value and losses on enterprises based on their own assessments, and therefore sign strict restrictive pacts.

2.4.1.2 Risk loans

Risk loans provide financing support for the development of technology-based SMEs(small and medium-size enterprises). The US risk loans originated in the 1960s and now has accounted for about 10%-20% of the size of the US venture capital market. After decades of development, venture loans have become an important source of financing for U.S. start-ups, technology-based SMEs in particular. About three quarters of start-ups use risk loans to acquire funding. Of every 7 dollars in venture capital, 1 dollar is obtained through risk loans.

Venture loan is a bond financing model. Technology-based SMEs, especially start-ups, have difficulty in obtaining traditional loans from banks due to insufficient or even lack of funds and mortgage assets. Risk loans, however, provide opportunities for these enterprises. Technology-based SMEs or start-ups obtain risk loans from professional banks or non-bank financial institutions to raise funds, while transferring warrants or stock options to financial institutions to compensate for high risks from loans. Compared with venture capital, venture loans are a relatively new financing method. It is also an important financing method for start-up technology-based SMEs, Risk loans in the United States are divided into bank risk loans and non-bank risk loans. There are a total of 30 institutions engaged in risk loans, predominantly 4 banks and 9 non-bank financial institutions. Among the banks that carry out risk lending, Silicon Valley Bank is the main risk loan bank, and also the largest risk loan bank. Its business accounts for 70% of all risk banking operations in the United States. Among the non-bank risk loan institutions, Encore Capital Corporation is a venture loan institution from the beginning. Western Technology Investment Corporation has the largest volume of venture loan business (more than 100 orders per year). Three Point Capital is the very loan institution that provides risk loans to Facebook and YouTube.

In the field of venture loan banking, the most famous is Silicon Valley Bank (SVB). Founded in 1983, Silicon Valley Bank is part of the SVB Financial Group. After years of development, Silicon Valley Bank has successfully embarked on a path for commercial banks to serve technology-based SMEs, thus forming a unique and mature business operation model. During the financial crisis in 2008, Silicon Valley Bank played an active role in helping technology-innovated companies to weather difficult times. It turned out to be profitable throughout the financial crisis.

The main successful experience of Silicon Valley Bank lies in the following five aspects.

1.Clear strategic positioning, and sure of the industry which it concentrates on supporting

In terms of strategic positioning, Silicon Valley Bank has a different approach from other banks, highlighting its support for technology-based SMEs. Silicon Valley Bank has explicitly proposed to focus on supporting high-tech industries, and customers are clearly located in technology-based SMEs with venture capital support but not yet listed, especially newly-established technology-based SMEs that the high-tech industry has concentrated on supporting, are developing at a faster pace and are considered to be risky by banks. Long-term technology-based enterprises serving specific industries enables Silicon Valley Bank to accurately grasp the characteristics and market value of these technology-based enterprises, thereby effectively reducing the degree of asymmetrical information between banks and enterprises.

2.Provide financing and value-added services to start-up companies at different stages and in different industries

Silicon Valley Bank divides start-ups into three stages and sets up independent business groups to provide them with different financial services. The first is the accelerating period. The company is in its infancy or at the early development stage, and the products are still in the process of research and development. There is no sales revenue or sales are small-scale, less than \$5 million. At this stage, Silicon Valley

Bank mainly provides mid-to-long-term entrepreneurship loans and matches them with the start-up investment capital absorbed by enterprises to support enterprises in completing research and development of products and achieve external sales. The second is the growth stage. At this time, the company's products have hit the market, and the sales revenue is increasing, between $5 million and $75 million. Silicon Valley Bank mainly provides enterprises with running capital loans required for business development. Generally, supply chain financing products such as account pledge are used. The third is the corporate finance stage. At this time, the sales scale of the company has exceeded $75 million. Silicon Valley Bank mainly provides cash management and global financial management solutions to the company.

On the basis of segmented industries, Silicon Valley Bank provides exclusive services to start-ups. Silicon Valley Bank mainly focuses on high-tech fields such as information technology, life sciences and clean energy, and traditional industries such as high-end wines. It assembles professional marketing teams in different sub-sectors and fields, and uses their accumulated professional knowledge to provide them with financing services. As of the end of 2010, the loan balances were $5.5 billion. Of the 45% information technology company loans, 33% were software, 12% were communications, semiconductors and electronics and other hardware, 10% were life sciences company loans, 8% were high-end wine and clean energy company loans, 19% were start-up investment fund loans, and 10% were private bank loans. Among information technology and life science industry loans, business loans at the accelerating stage accounted for 14%, business loans at the growth stage accounted for 59% (of which factoring financing accounted for 11%), corporate finance stage loans accounted for 14%, and M & A loans accounted for 13%.

In addition to providing financial support, Silicon Valley Bank Financial Group also provides diversified value-added services to start-ups to help them achieve entrepreneurial success and form a win-win situation for enterprises, start-up investment and banks. Establishing a corporate entrepreneurship platform under the bank is to provide various services for start-ups. The business is focused on directly exchanging with early entrepreneurship, gives them unique banking experience and services, and provides enterprises with CFO training through various forms to improve their management ability, introduces investors to enterprises to assist firms in completing equity financing. In 2010, about 1,100 CEOs of start-ups participated in entrepreneurial platform service activities organized by Silicon Valley Bank.

3.Renewed fund resources

After investigation, Silicon Valley Bank found that 21% of the US GDP was created by establishment supported by venture capital companies. Many very successful ones have received the support of venture capital companies. Therefore, Silicon Valley Bank pays special attention to cooperation with venture capital companies when providing financial support to technology companies. The main business of Silicon Valley Bank is to provide commercial banking services for enterprises invested by venture capital institutions. Silicon Valley Bank does not directly invest in the equity of technology-based SMEs, but indirectly invests in them through granting loans to venture capital companies. Banks will also provide direct banking services to venture capital institutions, such as banks providing financial services like account opening and fund entrust; banks will set up branches near venture capital institutions in order to provide them with timely services. Silicon Valley Bank also directly invests in more than 200 venture capital funds, becoming their shareholders or partners, and establishing a more solid foundation of cooperation between banks and customers. Silicon Valley Bank established a venture capital advisory committee to ensure close contact with venture capital. These efforts have enabled Silicon Valley Bank and venture capital to weave a network of relationships in which everyone can share information, carry out deeper cooperation, and jointly support the development of start-ups.

The development of financial technology in Silicon Valley Bank has been promoted through cooperation with venture capital institutions. Through cooperation with venture capital institutions, the customer identification can be more reasonable. Silicon Valley Bank stipulates that all customers of the bank must be enterprises supported by venture capital, and they must sign a contract with the customer to hold patent technology and intellectual property as a pledge. In other words, Silicon Valley Bank makes a secondary selection of customers selected by venture capital institutions to improve customer quality during the customer access phase.

Low capital cost is gained through cooperation with venture capital institutions. Silicon Valley Bank does not absorb public deposits, but it has extensively absorbed the funds of venture capital investors, mainly because venture capital investors are not sensitive to deposit interest rates. About 30% of deposits are demand accounts, making the overall low cost of funds. Based on the high profitability of technology-based SMEs at the market expansion stage, the interest rates of Silicon Valley Bank loans to technology-based SMEs are, in general, high. Higher interest rates gap allows Silicon Valley banks to earn higher returns.

Cope with unfavorable market environment through cooperation with venture capital institutions. When the economy is falling, investors' investment enthusiasm drops sharply. At this time, Silicon Valley Bank further cooperates closely with venture capital institutions to deal with the unfavorable market environment.

4.Flexible use of equity and debt

From the perspective of the development stage of SMEs in the United States, debt financing was mainly relied on during the infancy and initial development of adolescents, which gradually declined after the SMEs matured. Equity financing, however, is just the opposite. The proportion of equity financing for SMEs in infancy and youth is not high, and after the company gradually grows, it relies heavily on equity financing. For debt investment, Silicon Valley Bank mainly draws some funds from the clients' funds. Although most funds for venture capital come from the sale of bonds and stocks, Silicon Valley Bank will draw a part from the clients' funds as capital to reduce the amount of funds raised and the expenditure required for the fundraising. After that, the bank invests funds in start-ups in the form of loans. When using equity investment, Silicon Valley Bank signs an agreement with the start-up to receive equity or stock options in order to profit from the exit. It is worth noting that Silicon Valley Bank often uses a mixture of two methods in its investments: one is lending funds to start-ups, and charging higher interest rates than the general borrowing in the market; the other is reaching agreements with start-ups to obtain some of their equity or options, which are generally 1%-2% of the total corporate share capital, are held by Silicon Valley Bank Financial Group and exercised when the company is publicly listed or acquired.

5.Rigorous risk control

Silicon Valley Bank mainly serves various start-ups, which face risks at the early and middle stages of development. However, the bad debt rate of Silicon Valley Bank is kept at a low level, which did not exceed 1% in 2010. The main reason is that Silicon Valley Bank has rigorously and effectively controlled risks. The first is to strengthen risk management by various means to control risks to the greatest extent.

Silicon Valley Bank has established a professional marketing team based on stages and industries. They can quickly diagnose and analyze the risks of the company to effectively identify risks and propose practical risks control measures because they are familiar with the market and sub—sectors of the company. At the same time, Silicon Valley Bank leverages external forces such as venture capital funds to conduct comprehensive analysis and judgment on client companies' entrepreneurial teams and other aspects to strengthen risk management.

Based on more than 10 years of historical data, Silicon Valley Bank has developed a credit risk rating model and adjusted it regularly every year. Based on this, it performs asset portfolio and risk pricing to achieve an organic match between risks and return. For example, the loan risks of early projects are relatively high. Silicon Valley Bank reduces the risks by reducing the amount of loans to start-up enterprises. Currently, the loan amount for early projects only accounts for about 10%. Take another example. In addition to providing financial support to high-tech companies at the early and middle stages, Silicon Valley Bank also issues loans to high-end wine companies and mature technology companies. The risks of financing these companies are low, and asset portfolios with different risk levels are used to effectively control credit risks.

Silicon Valley Bank strengthened risk management by strengthening cooperation with start-up investment funds. In order to reduce risks, Silicon Valley Bank generally requires that its loan customers must be enterprises supported by start-up investment funds. At the same time, it is very concerned about the intellectual property rights owned by startups. If the company cannot pay fees, it will work with the venture capital fund to sell the company's technology patent, and the proceeds they get will be repaid to the bank first to reduce the bad debt losses the bank faces.

2.4.2 Japan

The development of Japan's financial technology is a combination of government-oriented and bank-led models, with bank-led characteristics being more prominent. Japan's support for technology-based SMEs is mainly in the following areas.

1.Establish policy-based financial institutions to provide loan services and combine them with private financial institutions

Since the 1950s, the Japanese government has used the financial funds as the main source of funds to set up policy-based financial institutions such as the Japan Development Bank, the Central Bank of Commercial and Industrial Portfolio, the National Life Finance Corporation, the SME Finance Corporation, and the SME Credit Insurance Corporation, whose main sources of funding are government grants, fiscal borrowing, and bond issuance. Although they have different divisions of labor, their goals and objectives are basically the same, which is to provide loans and financial services for corporate scientific and technological innovation by using more preferential interest rates, loan terms and financing conditions than commercial financial institutions to ensure that corporate innovation receives adequate financial support, and to solve the fund problem in the development of SMEs.

Technology-based SME financing is mainly sourced from government financial institutions such as banks. Generally speaking, Japan provides indirect financing such as bank loans only after high-tech projects has entered a mature development stage. Providing funding for early-stage high-tech projects is primarily start-up investment firms, which are set in the banking and securities industries, often as members of a corporate group. In addition to government financial institutions, private financial institutions in Japan are also an important source of funding for high-tech SMEs. These institutions mainly provide loans to their members (SMEs) and local SMEs. When providing financing to SMEs, they can also receive support from multiple parties, including policy-based financial treasuries.

Japanese private small and medium-sized financial institutions and their branches are numerous and widely distributed, mainly including urban banks, local banks, second local banks, credit portfolios, credit vaults, and labor vaults. After the financial crisis in 2008, Japanese financial institutions have undergone a large-scale transformation. As of now, there are 6 large metro banks, 19 trust banks, 106 local banks, 57 foreign banks, and other banks, of which 6 urban banks occupy a dominant position in financial system in Japan. Its main business is absorbing deposits and providing loans to large enterprises. The deposits absorbed by metro banks account for about 20% of all Japanese banks' total deposits, of which corporate deposits account for about 60%. The headquarters of local banks are located in large and medium-sized cities, and their branches are widely distributed in prefectures and counties centered on the city where the headquarters are located. The main business of local banks is to absorb deposits from local individuals and small and medium-sized enterprises, mainly providing loans to local SMEs. Local banks have 7,500 branches and 35,000 ATMs across the country. Numerous dense branches enable local banks to cater to SMEs with different needs. They can provide financial services to many local SMEs, providing 70% loans of its total.

The early mutual banks in Japan in 1989 gradually turns the second local bank, which now has 42 member banks, 3133 branches, absorbs 56.099 billion yen in deposits, and 43.587 billion yen in loans. Its main functions are to actively promote local economic development, provide diverse financial services to local SMEs and individuals, and improve the quality of public financial services through cooperation with local finance.

Credit treasury is a local SME financial institution established on the basis of the Credit Treasury Law introduced in 1951. Its predecessor was a credit mutual cooperative. The credit treasury adopts the membership system, and members participating in the credit vault are only limited to employees in the region and local SMEs. The main business scope of credit finance includes absorbing members and social deposits, providing loans, exchange business, securities investment and policy-based financial treasury business to members.

Credit portfolio is a mutual aid organization established on the Japanese SME Mutual Aid Cooperation Law introduced in 1949. Its members include local small and medium-sized individual businesses, individuals, etc. The credit portfolio has always adhered to the concept of mutual assistance, and its service objects and scopes are limited in this local place, providing financial assistance to local SMEs and individuals. After 1951, some credit portfolios were converted into Japanese non-governmental financial institution system with its advanced credit vaults, expanding financing channels for different Japanese companies, and offering solutions and ideas for the difficulty of technology-based SMEs financing. At the same time, private financial institutions has also made up for the deficiencies of government policy-based financial institutions, improved Japan's financial system, and became an integral part of the Japanese financial system.

2. Establish a policy-based guarantee institution and improve the credit guarantee system

In order to solve the guarantee problem in the technological innovation financing process of Japanese enterprises, especially SMEs, Japan has established a sound credit guarantee system. Japan's credit guarantee system is mainly composed of the Japan Credit Guarantee Association, the SME Credit Insurance Treasury, and the Chamber of Commerce and Industry. Credit Guarantee Associations and SME credit insurance vaults provide credit guarantees to SMEs when they apply for loans from commercial banks, or provide debt insurance for enterprises, reducing the risks of loan banks and credit guarantee associations. Through loan guarantees and related insurance systems and policy-based loans provided by the government, SMEs are provided with commercial bank loans at preferential market rates, greatly reducing the difficulty of financing SMEs.

The SME Credit Insurance Treasury is an institution that provides credit insurance for SME loan guarantees. SMEs guaranteed by the Credit Guarantee Association under the Credit Insurance Treasury can obtain 60 times of funds, which is much higher than that of other countries (multiple 10). In specific operations, SMEs can apply for guarantees from guarantee associations, and then the associations can arrange loans from financial institutions; they can also apply for loans from financial institutions, and financial institutions apply for guarantees from associations. SMEs pay a guarantee fee of 0.1% or 0.5% to the association after receiving the loan. The insurance treasury re-guarantees the credit guarantee association. When encountering the repayment difficulties of SMEs, the credit insurance association can obtain the equivalent of 70% to 80% of the loan repayment from the insurance treasury .

3.Improve laws and regulations and provide preferential policies for technology-based SMEs

The Japanese government established the National Small and Medium Business Administration in 1948, and regional SME bureaus and small and medium-sized business departments in administrative regions at all levels, establishing a complete information network for SMEs to provide good technology and fund information. In order to promote the development of high-tech industries and revitalize the Japanese economy, the Japanese government has introduced more than 30 laws and regulations directly related to SMEs, including not only the basic law, but also a number of supporting separate laws and regulations, clearing obstacles for SMEs investment.

In order to stimulate the development of the national economy, the Japanese government has used policies to reduce the conditions for the establishment of companies and for industry access to increase national entrepreneurial enthusiasm, especially SMEs. In 2003, the Japanese government reduced the company's registered capital to 1 yen and provided corresponding tax relief for SMEs. For example, for a venture company established by an individual within 10 years, the equity transfer revenue is taxed at 75%; SMEs with a pre-tax profit of less than 8 million yen are reduced by 8% compared with large enterprises, that is, corporate income is taxed at a rate of 22%; 7% of the tax is deducted for SMEs purchasing or renting machinery and equipment. Through the establishment of a special technology development subsidy system, a 50% financial subsidy is provided for the technology development of SMEs. In addition, in order to facilitate the information acquisition of SMEs and improve their technological level, the Japanese government has used financial subsidies to invest more than 3 billion yen in the construction of SME information networks and databases, and has been dynamically updated and adjusted them to help SMEs. to obtain relevant latest information and materials.

4.Promote the development of multi-layer capital market

Under the traditional financial system dominated by banks, Japans banking system has developed rapidly and dominated the entire financial system over the past few decades. Just because of this, the development of Japans securities market has been slower, and Japans capital market is far less developed than that of the United States. It was not until the 1980s that Japan carried out financial system reform, relaxed financial supervision, promoted the internationalization and liberalization of finance, and gradually realized the marketization of interest rates. Only then did Japans capital market develop rapidly, and the proportion of direct financing in corporate financing also increased slowly. After more than 30 years of development, Japan has gradually formed a multi-level capital market, and the developed level of the capital market has been third across the country. The developed capital market provides diversified and direct financing channels for the innovation and development of technology companies. The stock market, bond market, foreign exchange market, offshore financial market and financial spin-offs market form a multi-level capital market system together.

Japan's securities market is divided into four levels. The first and second levels are referred to as first market and second market, which represent the main board and small and medium board markets. The third board market, mainly targeted at emerging markets, is a major direct financing channel for high-tech company. The Jasdaq market established by Japan on the basis of the OTC market in 1998 was introduced after imitating Nasdaq, mainly for high-tech SMEs and venture capital companies. In 2004, the Japanese "Jasdaq" market was upgraded to a stock exchange. The OTC store market, together with the Jasdaq Stock Exchange, constitutes the fourth level of the Japanese stock market. In 1999, the Nagoya Stock Exchange established the "Growth Company Market". The Tokyo Stock Exchange established the "High Growth Emerging Stock Market" in the same year, and the Fukuoka

Stock Exchange established the Q-board market in 2000. The Tokyo Exchange's MOTHERS (Market of the High Growth and Emerging Stocks), the Osaka Stock Exchange's JASDAQ, Nagoya's Centrex, Fukuoka's Q-Board, and Sapporo's AMBITIOUS make up the Japanese GEM Market, providing direct financing channels for technology-based SMEs.

In addition, the bond market has also developed significantly after relaxed regulation, and the Japanese government has started allowing Japanese companies to issue unsecured corporate bonds in the capital market. The development of the capital market has changed the traditional financial system, providing more convenient conditions for the financing of technology-based enterprises, SMEs in particular, and providing more choices for venture capital investment to exit from technology-based enterprises after equity investment. Since then, the Japanese wave of starting a business has dawned. As a result, the Japanese economy has enjoyed a long-term recovery and development.

5.Improved venture capital market

Japan established a venture capital financial institutions as early as the 1950s. However, since they were established by the government, it is called a "venture capital bank", still the first venture capital company in Japan to provide low-risk companies with low-interest loans. The establishment of Japanese venture capital institutions is influenced by American venture capital firms. However, due to Japan's unique bank-dominated financial system, the organizational forms and funding sources of venture capital institutions are not the same as those in the United States. Japan's venture capital has gone through three stages: the initial development stage (from the 1950s to the 1970s), the adjustment stage (1974-1982), and the comprehensive development stage (from 1983 to the present). A sound venture capital market has now been formed. The Japanese government has provided a comprehensive legal guarantee for the development of venture capital through the formulation of a series of policies and regulations.

In the 1980s, Japan carried out reforms over financial systems and kept relaxing supervision. At that time, mixed financial holding companies began to form, which began to set up subsidiaries related to venture capital business. This type of venture capital company was once occupying the dominant position of Japanese venture capital, with the main businesses of providing guarantees, low-interest loans, purchasing stocks and transferable bonds. The remaining venture capital institutions still have a government-led official color. As a venture capital institution of a financial holding company subsidiary, due to the restriction of its affiliation, venture capital institutions cannot completely pursue development with the goal of maximizing profits. Instead, considering financial institutions own development, venture capital funds will be invested in companies with lower risks for the pursuit of relatively stable returns, which has led to difficulties in financing for technology-based SMEs at the early stages.

In 1994, the government started a comprehensive plan to support the development of venture capital. Through the improvement of technology, talents, and the market, the software and hardware environment of venture capital was reformed under the guidance of policies. mainly including: Formulating policies and regulations to support the development of venture capital, such as the Angel Investor Tax System introduced in 1997 which provides tax incentives for angel investors who qualify for technology-based SMEs; Repealing restrictions on sending managers to technology-based SMEs, making venture capital institutions dispatch of managers to technology-based enterprises possible, which relatively lowers the risk of venture capital enterprises, and promotes the equity investment behavior of them.

In 1995, Japan enacted the "Small and Medium Enterprises Creative Activities Promotion Law", which established a total of 50 billion yen in venture capital funds through SME groups, which were provided to private venture capital companies by various venture capital groups. In 1999, Japan formulated the "Angel Investment Tax System" and revised the regulations on the use of pension funds to allow individuals, foreign capital and pension funds to enter the venture capital industry and broaden the source of venture capital funds. In 1998, Japan learned from the United States and introduced the "Portfolio Law of Limited Investment Undertakings", which allows venture capital institutions to form a limited liability system. The Japanese government has set up a comprehensive support center for SMEs in the country to provide professional services for venture capital enterprises, including providing professional consulting for business management, entrepreneurial knowledge lectures, expert guidance and opening entrepreneurial forums. At the same time, Japan has established and improved the second-board market and over-the-counter market, correspondingly reduced market access conditions, made exit channels for venture capital unimpeded, which greatly make them more interested in venture capital. In 2005, Japan merged the three existing laws into the "Law on Promoting New Business Activities of Small and Medium-Sized Enterprises" to encourage and guide venture capital into high-tech industries.

Compared with the market-based technology financial model represented by the United States, the bank-based technology financial model in Japan has certain defects and limitations. The biggest flaw is that the income model of bank bond financing does not match the risk level of high-tech enterprises. The risks of high-tech enterprises are mainly concentrated on the earliest stages of enterprises and production of products, and often the risks are relatively large. However, bank loans often require stable loan interest and relatively low risk. Therefore, this asymmetry and incompatibility lead to market failure. Thus the government-led technology financial model often requires government intervention. The implementation of government technology finance related policies will exert a great impact on the country's financial technology development level.

1.Create a macroeconomic environment and provide relevant preferential policies

Since 1993, the British government has successively promulgated "Exploiting Our Potential: Science, Engineering and Knowledge-Driven Economy", "Science and Innovation", "Excellence and Opportunity-Science and Technology Innovation Policy for the 21st Century", "Enterprises, Skills and Innovation", "Science and Innovation Strategy", "Our Opportunities in a Changing World", and "Development Strategies for Innovation Investment in Science, Engineering and Technology". These series of white papers have laid the foundation for financial technology development in UK.

In February 1994, the British government launched the ROPA scheme (Reward Scheme for Exploring Our Potential), which rewards scientists who are willing to engage in long-term cooperative projects, and promises to provide 3.5 million pounds of incentive funds in the first financial year to promote interaction between university and business scientists. In addition, an increase of 600, 000 in the CASE award scheme was mainly used to fund postgraduate to carry out research projects in enterprises. The British government launched the Faraday Partnership Program in 1997, which connected business with academia to closely link research institutions in related research fields with relevant researchers in enterprises (especially SMEs) to conduct research in related directions, which will share risks, and results, benefit both parties, and allow academic research to be better transformed into scientific and technological achievements, and be applied to the scientific and technological innovation of SMEs. The "Forecast-Link" award scheme established in 1998 aims to increase technological competitiveness of SMEs by linking enterprises, especially SMEs, with universities and scientific research institutions to innovate financial technology in response to market demand. The "University Challenge Plan" launched in 2000 also serves the same purpose to encourage universities to establish links with corporate research and development institutions, to transform scientific research results into applicable commercial results at the early stages of corporate R & D, and to achieve the win-win interests of academia and enterprises. In 2001, the British Council for Higher Education Funds and the Office of Science and Innovation established the Higher Education Innovation Fund, which specializes in providing funding for research results used by higher education institutions to support enterprises and industry sectors, with the aim of strengthening the relationship between enterprises and universities, promoting the transformation of scientific research results, and providing technical support for technology-based SMEs.

In addition, the British government also provides a number of tax incentives for technology-based enterprises, especially SMEs. In order to promote the equity capital financing of SMEs in the start-up period, the British government introduced the Enterprise Investment Scheme (ES) in 1994 to provide tax relief for investors, mainly including income tax reduction and capital gains tax exemptions, capital loss reductions, and delayed tax for investors accompanying the issuance and sale of stocks to encourage investment. The revenue expenditures for scientific and technological development can be regarded as general operating expenses and can be deducted from the operating income before tax, an equivalent of the exemption of income expenditures for technological development. Science and technology research expenses paid by enterprises to research institutions (including universities, research institutes, etc.) and to engage in business operations can be deducted before tax; tax deduction for capital expenditures on scientific and technological development, that is, capital expenditures used by companies on technology development, which can be deducted from income before taxes by 10%. In addition, companies investment in scientific research equipment, laboratory buildings, intellectual property rights and technological skills, can enjoy tax relief for science and technology development. Through these tax reduction and exemption policies, the British government stimulated the enthusiasm of science and technology enterprises to engage in science and technology development, and relieved a considerable part of the financial burden on technology-based.

2.Provide direct financial assistance and credit guarantees for SMEs

In 1991, the British Government Chancellor of the Exchequer Brown announced the "Knowledge Budget" plan. The budget announced that companies with an annual profit of less than 100,000 pounds will reduce the initial tax rate of 10% on corporate taxes; small and medium-sized companies received 12.5% tax subsidies to prevent them from reducing investment in research and development in order to pay taxes; the government will provided 20 million pounds of venture capital cooperation funds to newly established high-tech companies; the government implemented a tax exemption plan for managers who have worked in small high-tech companies for three consecutive years to solve the problem of small companies' inability to attract management talent due to lack of funds; Large venture capital companies can enjoy tax-free treatment from government.

The British government has also formulated various reward schemes to reward SMEs actively participating in technological innovation. For example, the British government passed the Small Business Research and Technology Development Award Scheme (SMART Program) in 1997 to provide 45,000 pounds of funding for research on technological innovation in small businesses with less than 50 people to support R & D of small business; for small businesses with less than 250 employees, the government also grants a maximum of 200,000 pounds for development before new products and technologies are produced.

In 1999, the UK Department of Trade and Industry also invested an additional 26 million pounds to establish the second round of "Small Enterprise Product Development Reward Scheme (SPUR Scheme)" to reward long-term technological innovation of small and medium-sized manufacturing enterprises. In 2004, the Ministry of Trade and Industry launched the "Technology Plan" to encourage enterprises to develop and apply targeted technologies.

In November 2004, the Department of Trade and Industry released a five-year plan on creating wealth with knowledge, announcing that it will reduce the 1 billion capital burden for enterprises within 10 years, thereby helping high-tech enterprises get development and help, especially technology-based SMEs. In 2008, the Department of Trade and Industry invested 3.36 billion pounds in technological innovation, accounting for 59.4% of its financial expenditure.

The British Government launched the British Small Business Loan Guarantee Scheme (SFIG) in 1981, which was managed by the Small Business Services Department (SBS) under the Department of Trade and Industry (DT) and was implemented by government funds, financial institutions and other lenders. The purpose of the SFIG plan is to promote the development of SMEs in the UK through government loan guarantees, especially those that have viable development plans and technical routes, but have difficulty financing for lack of funds or repayment of loans. The Department of Trade and Industry provides loan guarantees for these SMEs. They can obtain bank loans of up to 100, 000 pounds to get out of trouble or sustain development through government guarantees, and the loan repayment period is 2-7 years. If the guaranteed SMEs are ultimately unable to repay the loan, the Department of Trade and Industry will accordingly bear 70% of the loan repayment and pay 2.5% annual interest.

3.Establish and improve a multi-level capital market

The United Kingdom is a large venture capital country, which mainly supports SME financing by creating SME financing platforms. The British Second-Board Market is the London Stock Exchange Alternative Investment Market (AIM), which was established on June 19, 1995, a national market provided by the London Stock Exchange for UK and overseas start-up, high-growth companies. From the establishment of the AIM to the beginning of the 21st century, more than 850 companies have achieved tremendous growth through AIM, with cumulative capital raised of more than 6.2 billion pounds, equivalent to 9.7 billion euros. The UK unlisted company stock trading market (ie, the third-board market) was founded on October 2, 1995, with the purpose of establishing a market for the sale of their stocks and shares for companies that have not entered the main board market of the London Stock Exchange or.

Chapter 3 Supervision of Financial Technology

Overall situations, financial technology does not change the nature and functions of finance. Despite changed carrier, channel and technology of financial transactions and improved transaction efficiency, financial technology does not really change the objects of transactions or the nature of finance. In terms of financial functions, Robert Merton, Nobel Laureate in Economics, points out that the financial system has six basic core functions: the function of clearing and payment settlement, the function of aggregating and allocating resources, the function of transferring resources between different time and space, the function of managing risks, the function of providing information, and the function of addressing incentive problems. No matter how financial technology changes the financial carrier, channel and technology, the above functions of the financial system remain the same. Be it financial technology or internet finance, its essence is still finance, and it is still functioning.

Financial technology poses new risks, therefore transforming requirements about financial regulation. Financial technology has the same moral hazard and adverse selection as traditional finance. The same is true of financial technology when it comes to institution and business. It faces credit risks, market risks, operation risks, liquidity risks, and reputation risks. At the same time, due to the technological factors contained in financial technology, its risks come in new forms and characteristics. The universality of financial technology, on the one hand, strengthens the externality of finance. Financial technology contributes significantly to advancing inclusive finance, but the "long tail" people it serves are the disadvantaged groups. What's worse, unicorn companies even develop into systemically important institutions, giving rise to an array of problems too big and sensitive to fail. Innovation of financial technology, on the other hand, puts risks of information technology under the spotlight. Technology loopholes, management defects, and human factors can paralyze the system and interrupt organization's operations. The United States Financial Stability Oversight Council (FSOC) has regarded IT (information technology) security as a major risk affecting financial stability. In general, financial risks inherent in financial technology are more complex and hidden. Furthermore, information technology risks and financial externalities are becoming more prominent, and financial technology faces more complex potential systematic and cyclical risks.The supervision of financial technology, to some extent, is related to technology. The supervision of financial technology, to some extent, is related to technology. This classic proposition shows that, the more intelligent and technical financial technology is, the governance and supporting mechanisms are more needed to ensure that the neutral concepts of technology and the Internet are more closely related to "finance" and "externalities". In other words, in order to grasp the development of financial technology and improve the efficiency of financial services and ensure its innovation vitality, it is necessary for us to introduce a reasonable and effective regulatory balance to promote its development. That is why every country's financial technology sector requires regulatory arrangements. Regulation ensures its healthy development and helps solve major problems.

3.1 Development of supervision technology

Everyone may have heard of financial technology, but rarely are familiar with the term supervision technology. It is less popular with people than financial technology. The word, however, emerged in the West in 2013. Specialized supervision technology summit appeared at that time. In March 2015, the scientific adviser of the British government once stated in a report that financial technology may be used for supervision and compliance, making financial supervision and report more transparent and efficient. We can use technology to establish a new supervision technology mechanism, which is the origin of financial supervision technology.

Many who carry out research about supervision technology take the 2008 financial crisis as the demarcation point. The advantage is that the demarcation is obvious, but the disadvantage is that it has nothing to do with technology. If it is based on the demarcation before development of financial technology, the technology before advancement is mainly used to analyze transactions, like warning of abnormal transactions in the stock exchange. As science and technology gain steam, however, we should further improve laws and regulations, establish rules, and develop towards the review of know your digit finance and financial supervision.

Period 1.0 (1987-2008)

It was at the point that global financial institutions' M&A reached their highest peak. As a result of expanding financial institutions across fields or sectors, the challenges of internal operations and financial supervision continued to increase and risk management and regulatory compliance of financial institutions became increasingly expanded. Since 1980, financial measurement in the financial field has grown at an eye-popping speed and IT industry has risen, making financial institutions rely heavily on computers on risk management, like financial transaction risks. Regulators, in the same vein, supervise financial institutions by quantitative risk management, like BASEL regulation.

Period 2.0 (2008-2019)

Since the financial crisis in 2008, supervision institutions around the world have begun to carry out large-scale and intensive supervision reforms, those related to legal compliance in particular. The exchange of information and the management of quantitative risks, therefore, have held the key. This move has not only, to a large extent, evolved relevant information technology but also, to a considerable extent, hit global financial institutions, demanding a strict attitude towards risk management and regulatory compliance. Traditional financial institutions, notably large global banks, have also become important pioneers in legal compliance.

Period 3.0 (after 2019)

In the future, supervision technology will consist of three development directions. The first is from KYC to KYD. Traditional KYC is achieved through real interpersonal interaction between the industry and customers. With the development of financial technology, customer identity verification and credit record are realized through interaction of debt paying ability and through which risk orientation will be converted into computer technology from traditional ways. Second, financial supervision will be re-examined through the establishment of technology. As boundaries of financial institutions blur, supervision institutions will also re-examine the integration across industries and profound changes in the frontiers as well as changes in local conditions. They should, under the condition of effective establishment of supervision technology, promote the development of financial technology.

3.2 What is supervision technology?

Supervision technology can fall into two categories, according to different functions. One is legal compliance technology. The other is regulatory technology .

The first is legal compliance technology, from the perspective of the supervised. For example, in an attempt to meet the development needs of the supervision office, the financial institutions such as banks use new technologies to enhance their ability to operate risks in a legally-complaint way. The second is regulatory technology, from the perspective of regulators. For example, the supervision institution shall formulate supervision standards and evade supervision arbitrage for financial innovation behaviors brought by the application of new technologies to supervision objects, and use new technologies to improve the ability and efficiency of managers.

Law compliance technology was developed by financial institutions so as to meet regulatory compliance and requirements. It is divided into two categories.

The first is the increased costs such as the regulation and rules.

Recent years have witnessed rapid growth of smart technologies, such as artificial intelligence, blockchain, machine learning, big data, cloud technology, and the internet of things. They have been applied to finance to generate financial technology. But in terms of supervision and management, they, are also learning to use technology to achieve compliance and legal requirements. Internationally, for example, Banque BNP Paribas was fined \$ 8.9 billion by the U.S. supervisory authority for anti-money laundering issues. Deutsche Bank was fined \$ 629 million by the British and US authorities for failing to meet the standards. Citigroup added 30,000 employees in 2014 for compliance.

For these finance-related technologists, they also began to learn the laws and regulations by which the financial industry operates and tried to understand the reasons why these regulations and management were formulated. To the surprise of the technical entrepreneurs, the rapid changes and costs confused them facing changes. Only by investing in research and development early and by developing technology that complies with regulations can the cost of supervision be reduced while law compliance technology was sold to financial institutions and management units.

The second is that supervised institutions adopt financial technology to raise requirements for supervision technology.

Banks are institutions which operate risk. After the financial crisis in 2008, the risk changes confronted by banks increased. Financial transaction opponents covered everything from traditional offline business to online business to increased long-distance remote business. Loans gradually moved towards light guarantees and were unsecured, according to the 20/80 principle and the introduction of the long-tail theory, which were a radical departure from traditional bank risk management concepts. If banks rely merely on traditional tools and cannot fully forecast the risks, they, however, need the assistance of financial technology.

This change can be seen from the first point credit risk. With the development of new technology, traditional analysis credit risk methods for financial data, such as the use of the z-score model to analyze the probability of failure and big data exploration and text exploration, have turned into using artificial intelligence and big data to perform early warning before events and timely monitoring during events. Consequently, various risk management ways will significantly change. This change can also be seen from the second point liquidity risk. Online financial wealth management products being applied, customers' investment needs both high returns and high liquidity. They don't know, however, they are contradictory. This change can also be seen from the third point operation risks. Criminals use new technologies, such as Trojan horses, and hacking technology to steal customers' funds, generating the risk of fraud. One example is that hackers exploit remote controlled ATM to steal bank funds. Another example is that there are defects in design or business processes about financial products, which give rise to process risks.

These new technologies bring profits to commercial banks, but will also pose a profound threat to risk management. If not handled properly, they will incur great losses in reputation and regulatory fines.

From the perspective of supervision institutions, the reasons are on several fronts.

The first is the traditional supervision. Traditional supervision institutions will check the credit risk, market risk, liquidity risk and operational risk of financial institutions. And, during the supervision process of banks, the CBRC (China Bank Regulatory Commission) has also formulated risk management rules covering these areas. The regulations, including various policies and measures on the trading company governance of related parties and separation of property and economics, pose specific requirements for comprehensive risk management of banking financial institutions. In 2012, the Basel Committee revised the core principles of effective bank supervision, and refined and segmented the standards of the risk management system.

The second is the supervision of financial technology. Financial technology banks have spawned 4 features: virtual online accounts, online transactions, immediate capital flow, and remote customers identification. The network improves the efficiency of financing, the real risks are, however, still difficult to identify. Some over-packaged innovative products, risk transmission, and wider implication, make the financial industry itself completely different. Financial practitioners must understand the technology of financial technology, and at the same time explore the source of financial problems and the process of transmission. In addition, financial fraud, anti-money laundering, network security and other toxic substances generated by financial technology have created new challenges for traditional supervision. In order to adapt to the changes of the new market and promote the healthy development of financial behaviors, the supervision department must keep pace with the times and promote the application and innovation of new technology of supervision institutions.

The supervision technologies can fall into four categories PwC (PricewaterhouseCoopers) divides the types of supervision technology into four categories. The first is efficiency and cooperation, the second integration of standard and understanding, the third prediction learning simplification, and the fourth the new direction.

The first category is efficiency and cooperation. The supervision technology can enable different areas of the financial industry to make progress, and help improve the presentation of supervision reports on the levels of efficiency cooperation. After the 2008 financial crisis, great changes have taken place in supervision environment. Supervision institutions across the countries responded by introducing a series of supervision measures, covering market infrastructure, investment institutions, and individuals looking at overall risks. Subsequently, the types and quantities of data that financial institutions needed to provide to regulators increased sharply. Financial institutions needed to integrate compliance procedures by new technologies, thereby improving compliance efficiency and reducing costs. Supervision technology provides companies with more flexibility in establishing data collection, which can lower the cost and lighten the burden of supervision reports.

In addition, due to legal compliance and internal control, the cost and mentality of the investment are gradually increasing. Domestic financial institutions have suffered misleading losses due to staff cheat, external fraud, and appropriate internal control. And, the suggestions by the administration are that they should give advice, according to everything they hear and see. In Jinfengyuan's assessment, internal control is not the responsibility of a single unit. Risk control can be divided into three parts.

The first defense is the person most directly at risk. It is also the goalkeeper of the three lines of defense that can prevent risks before they occur. Bank clerks, for instance, assist customers in all business relationships and find that customers often deposit large amounts of money for others. When entering or leaving a specific account, you should accept the investigation with the legal department and declare the transaction, according to regulations, which, however, is suspected of money laundering.

The second defense should strengthen the communication with the first one, as well as cooperation with the third. It should also deepen understanding of the business and investigate based on the refusal and the rights collection. During this time, technology can function as the first step. The defense function of the second defense is to use the sharing platform to share common methods, various risk files, and monitor related data.

In addition, the supervision institutions demand frequent changes. Supervisors will regularly modify their needs, and spend more energy in updating records. Cloud technology is flexible enough to respond to changes in supervision through more efficient data sharing, cooperative remote access. Also, it can help the team perform risk assessment and report. In order to meet the needs of updating and upgrading, cloud technology can provide low-cost applications, that is, an effective model for responding to the requirements of corresponding supervision. Based on these attributes, cloud technology plays a crucial part in long-term supervision.

The second is the integration of standards and understanding. The standards and understanding of supervision technology in compliance with regulations can provide assistance and improvement, such as establishment and analysis of models applied to technology and data points, use of artificial intelligence technology to develop regulatory analysis capabilities and rules of their intention, which will facilitate automation, significantly reduce the cost of change, and ensure consistency in regulations and performance.

For identification of fraud, based on historical data, for example, machine learning tools can effectively identify possible fraud, and be used in the field of anti-money laundering and counter-terrorism financing as well as transaction monitoring. Machine learning has improved language and text processing capacity. Once there is a transaction behavior that deviates from compliance requirements, the system will automatically alert financial institutions to help financial institutions to meet compliance requirements more effectively.

On the application interface, the application interface technology not only provides a financial data interaction standard, but can also perform on-demand transactions. With the opening of financial institutions and supervision institutions, sharing application interfaces, establishing reports and inspections based on public data, and monitoring suspicious anti-money laundering and payment fraud will be made more efficient. Specifically, we will digitize various supervision policies and regulations with programmable requirements. Supervision institutions provide supervision APIs for financial institutions to facilitate financial institutions to programme their internal processes, and yield reports by exchange of data through a unified API protocol. The above can increase integration and interoperability between application systems in an attempt to reduce costs, increase efficiency, and promote platform innovation.

In terms of data sharing, the new encryption security technology can share information on the basis of protecting privacy and ensuring the security and integrity of data. At the same time, it can improve the efficiency of information disclosure of financial institutions to supervisory agencies. Emerging information sharing and encryption technology allow individuals to provide relevant encrypted information according to access authorization, and to mark raw data by attributes, objects, and access types, thereby greatly reducing the processing work on raw data of financial institutions, and more effectively disclosing information. Even under large amounts of data, new encryption technologies can also be mapped to common data platforms through access control to help institutional customers with their data security issues, enabling data to be shared with supervision agencies, and sharing supervision's data routines and structures, which can promote efficiency, reduce costs, and simplify interaction.

The third is the simplified prediction learning. From the perspective of risk compliance monitoring and for the financial industry, the biggest advantage of developing technology is that it can digitize the paper reporting process, reduce the supervisions human cost and centralization, meet the supervision requirements, and effectively reduce costs. Supervision technology can help financial institutions to seamlessly connect systems, set up supervisory policies, conduct self-tests and verify business operations in a timely manner, and complete the active identification and control of risks. It can also promptly reduce the risks, identification risks and fraud through the correlation and calculation of information from different sources.

In the past few years of machine learning, due to the requirements of supervision and the electronization of services, financial institutions have obtained a large amount of highly-frequent non-data structure information. Therefore, in the face of massive highly-frequent and low-quality data, supervision institutions and financial institutions urgently need strong analyzing tool. Artificial intelligence such as machine learning, coupled with other automated analysis technologies, emerged. Machine learning can enable supervision technology to better perform metaphors for situation analysis. With advanced analysis models and visualization technologies, companies can analyze data at more depth. Machine learning can also enable the supervision system to automatically re-evaluate, and complete the process through user feedback to replace more complex, large and repetitive supervision tasks. With the increase in the amount of data analysis, machine learning plays an increasingly important role in the supervision of financial institutions, and continues non-stop the use of data to meet compliance requirements for financial institutions and supervision units.

As for big data analysis and financial institutions modeling, the available data is quite large in its thickness and breadth. These data are not fully utilized and cannot be effectively and actively used for risk management. Big data supervision is based on dynamic and real-time interaction, and conducts systematic and forward-looking supervision of behaviors and potential risks in the financial system through financial big data. Under this circumstance, the supervision led by organizations such as local business is gradually weakened. As a result, the supervisor will more check the data and behaviors represented by data. Big data, with the help of effective analysis and presentation, not only can enable the supervisors to quickly notice what happened and what is happening but also can predict the imminent risks and their occurrence probability, which is more conducive for the supervisors to allocate resources. Supervision technology can use analysis tools to analyze existing data, and lock their potential use, so that the same data can be used for different purposes.

The fourth is new directions led by supervision technology, from distributed classification of blockchain and achieved compliance of biometrics with internals to blockchain and other distributed ledgers, and transaction platforms probably allowed between financial institutions in the future. It also includes an payment system and information sharing mechanism, especially when combined with biometric technology, which made digital identity promptly reduce costs, and understood customers' inspections in a reliable manner. In plain English, the blockchain is mainly about separate use of the database to multiple computers, making these databases impossible to be controlled by a single entity. At the same time, it protects the data in an encrypted manner, tracks payers and payees, and monitors transaction balances. This entire system is called distributed classification ledger technology.

As long as the bank or exchange confirms that certain bank or company does own funds or assets that are traded with another company or bank, the entire checkout time can be reduced to seconds. Transparent design enables blockchain to provide supervisory agencies with direct, timely and completely transparent supervision information. Since all transactions are recorded on the distributed ledger, the organization can conduct a comprehensive, secure, accurate and irreversible, very permanent audit trail. The near-real-time transaction data brought by blockchain technology enable supervisors to better analyze systemic risks, improve the efficiency of on-site and off-site inspections, so as to improve the integrity of system, increase transparency, and redefine data sharing.

In terms of biometric identification technology, customer identification refers to the fact that it is necessary to fully know the customer and ensure that his or her identity information is authentic, valid, and integrated before a financial institution provides financial services to him or her. Customer identification recognition is an important measure to achieve anti-fraud and anti-money laundering. Financial institutions can effectively discover, report and prevent suspicious transaction behaviors through verification of customer identity and understanding of business behaviors. In recent years, the Internet has found its way into everyones daily life. As a result, financial institutions can provide customers with more convenient financial services through the Internet. Virtuality, however, makes it more difficult for them to identify customer. Biometrics, by means of measuring the physical characteristics of people, can verify the identity in a more effective and robust way. Not only can it solve the identification problem presented by the Internet, but also improve the efficiency of customer identification.

The establishment of compliance supervision technology can help senior managers to use existing systems and data to generate compliance data reports more efficiently and flexibly. Supervision technology can more clearly interpret the norms, and better manage the efficiency of regulations in banks and other institutions. What's more, we can use it to develop the process of automatic reporting and analysis of cognitive technology big data. Artificial intelligence made financial institutions better understand the surface meaning of the regulations, and the integration of automated systematized regulations, thereby applying automated supervision strategies, and updating supervision rules automatically, which will reduce the overall compliance costs.

Practical examples of financial supervision technology

The first is Avalara, an American company specializing on taxation management, with a cumulative investment of US $ 319.63 million. He is an automated tax payment software provider, dedicated to providing enterprises with a comprehensive and automated cloud computing tax payment solution, helping companies of all sizes to pay taxes, including VAT and consumption tax, which saves these firms amounts of time to tackle tax problems by calculating taxes that should be paid without the help of the calculator or purchasing expensive hardware and software. In 2004, the company was founded on the Seattle, Washington, USA. The founder felt deeply sorry for having saw what American companies do contradict cost efficiency. They spent a lot of time in manually calculating taxes that should be paid, or solved the problem of taxpayers by purchasing expensive business equipment of hardware and software. He, therefore, decided to invest in related products and the research and development of services so as to provide enterprises with comprehensive and automated cloud computing to solve taxation problems, and at the same time tackle various tax problems.

The second is, Metricstram, a supplier of compliance management solutions. The legal compliance management software solutions developed by it provide a common framework and software. Automated information flow and evaluation enable enterprises to test, remedy, help preventing non-compliance incidents, which in turn will reduce compliance costs. Founded in 1999, the company is located in California, USA, in the market for providing forensic management solutions, with its goal of simplifying business management risk and compliance processes.

The third is Logrhythn, which was founded in 2003 in Colorado,

USA. The goal is not only to help companies meet the increasing demand for incident management proposals, but also to assist corporations and organizations in quickly detecting, responding to, and mitigating known and unknown threats. It provides information, and security incident management platforms, and analyzes the behaviors of internal users through its security incident management software and artificial intelligence mechanism, and consults related events.

3.3 Financial technology supervision principles and framework

3.3.1 G20 Digital Inclusive Finance Advanced Principles and Action Suggestions

The Group of Twenty (G20) recognizes the critical role of inclusive finance in moving towards innovative, dynamic, interconnected, and inclusive world economy. Over the decade, digital finance has succeeded in making financial services more available for those ranging from G20 to women, the poor, young people, the elderly, farmers, SMEs, and other consumer groups having no access to full services of non-G20 countries. Successful digital inclusive financial business models, new regulatory rules and methods, have emerged worldwide. Therefore, on the basis of the G20 Innovative Financial Inclusion Principles in 2010, the G20 Finance Ministers and Central Bank Governors' Meeting adopted in July 2016 G20 High-Level Principles for Digital Financial Inclusion set by Global Partnership for Financial Inclusion (CPFI).

The G20 High-Level Principles for Digital Financial Inclusion contains eight main principles:

(1) Advocate the use of digital technology to promote the development of inclusive finance.

(2) Achieve the right balance between innovation and risks in digit-

al inclusive finance.

(3)Build the right digital inclusive framework of financial legal regulation.

(4)Expand digital financial services infrastructure.

(5)Take responsible digital financial measures to protect consumers.

(6) Attach importance to the popularization of consumer digital technology knowledge and financial knowledge.

(7)Promote digital customer identification of financial services.

(8)Monitor the growth of digital inclusive finance and report in a timely manner. Relevant principles have been confirmed at the G20 Hangzhou Summit, which can be considered as the current basic principles guiding the development and supervision of global financial technology. Among the eight principles, seen from the supervision perspective, principle (3) : establish a regulatory framework and principle (5) : protect consumers are particularly important.

G20 hopes to promote digital inclusive financial actions in various countries based on the above eight principles. The government should play a key role in it. In 2017, the GPFI submitted reports on digital inclusive finance to countries at the G20 Central Bank Governors' Meeting. On the basis of the eight principles, 66 suggestions for actions were made. Of the 66 digital action proposals of inclusive finance, most of them were officially made at the international level for the first time, which have extremely important guiding significance for development direction in the future as well as supervision orientation of financial technology.

Build the right supervision framework

Based on the third principle of building the right supervision framework, a series of very important suggestions for actions are made.

The first is to establish a legal framework. That is to build a legal framework for digital inclusive finance, and stipulate thresholds for market participation (access requirements included), appropriate prudential conditions (such as capital and liquidity), market behaviors and integrity, consumer protection, anti-money laundering or counter-terrorism financing guarantee mechanisms, and bankruptcy mechanisms, etc.

The second is to allow trying innovation. This framework should allow the trial of innovative service to provide channels, products, services and business models. It is not necessary to fully comply with all regulatory requirements in the early stages of a pilot project, but it must ensure fair and balanced monitoring mechanisms and obligations for money laundering or counter-terrorism financing and ensure that no participant gains an inappropriate edge in the pilot.

The third is to guarantee fairness. That is to ensure that no matter what kind of technology institutions use, the same type of digital financial service providers should have the same rights and obligations. Clear and consistent standards are provided for market access thresholds (including new access institutions and foreign access institutions) and specific types of digital financial services. And the same regulatory approach is used for similar risks, and appropriate risk-oriented regulatory approaches are improved to promote competition and promote a fair, open and balanced competitive environment.

The fourth is to improve the law. On the one hand, assess all contents of digital inclusive finance in domestic and international laws, identify and address overlapping or contradictory parts, and gaps, obstacles or other obstacles in the access process. These include: financial services, payment systems, communications, competition, discrimination, identity, barriers to access digital financial services for groups without formal financial services, and obligations of agents and employees. On the other hand, develop easy-to-understand digital inclusive financial laws, regulations, and guidelines, while making it easier for the financial industry and consumers to know these laws and regulations (like gain access to other communication channels through publicly accessible websites). More importantly, ensure that the responsibilities of regulators are clearly described in the legal and regulatory framework for digital financial services and digital inclusive finance in general.

Fifth, enhance supervision capabilities. Improvement of the capacity of regulators under legal and regulatory framework in the digital inclusive finance is not only aimed at better understanding digital technologies (like learning programs from their peers through domestic or international training), but also at encouraging the use of digital technologies to improve their regulatory processes and ability.

Six is to strengthen international regulatory exchanges. That is to establish the sustainable legal and regulatory framework, and information exchange mechanisms on digital inclusive finance and have a regular exchange of supervision methods among G20 members, including contents related to risk management strategies and experience.

Protect consumer rights

Based on the fifth principle of taking responsible digital financial measures to protect consumers, a set of actions suggestions were made. Requirements for service providers stand out.

The first is to establish a legal and consumer protection framework. On the one hand, a stable legal framework is built to ensure the safety of customer funds held by service providers that are not carefully monitored (such as through trust accounts, deposit insurance mechanisms and supplementary insurance requirements). At the same time, in combination with projects targeting vulnerable groups, the relevant rules of digital financial services anti-fraud are further enforced rigorously and a reasonable claim pursuing mechanism is established. On the other hand, design a consumer protection framework for digital financial services that not only addresses specific risks of the digital environment but also reflects statistical and behavioral evidence as well as direct consumer information, such as data from free consumer hot lines, online forums, and complaints.

The second is to increase demand for service providers. Requirements can be divided into mandatory and encouraging categories. Mandatory categories include:

(1)Disclose terms, fees, commissions and other information, with clear and concise expressions and comparable contents

(2)Submit account statements reflecting transaction and fee details regularly

(3)Open a free customer service hotline

(4)Make sure the processing procedures and responsibilities for unauthorized transactions, erroneous transactions, and system interruptions

(5)Regulate loans and debt collection activities

(6)Guide consumers to use digital financial services correctly, effectively prevent personal data from being abused, leaked, tampered and damaged

(7) Provide official contact information (such as phone numbers and websites) for consumer consultation

(8) Train their agents and employees. Training contents should contain product characteristics, regulatory responsibilities, fair treatment of vulnerable groups lacking in financial services, claim pursuing processes and interpretation of information disclosure documents at the request of clients or in the case of language barriers. Encouraging cate-

gories include: service providers are encouraged to submit regular reports on complaint data of digital financial services .

In terms of balancing innovation within risks, G20 Innovative Inclusive Finance Original Period has made important suggestions such as communicating with regulators, and exploring digital currencies. It is necessary to create a regular information sharing mechanism and smooth communication channels between regulators and service providers, and encourage regulators and the industry to formulate a risk management strategy that reflects the specific conditions and legal framework of different jurisdictions such as being consistent with local conditions. That is "Know Your Customer" (KYC) rules rather than avoiding such consumers and accounts, and exploring the benefits for inclusive finance of digital legal currencies, and so so.

In terms of promoting identity recognition, the G20 Principles of Innovative Inclusive Finance makes important data opening and tiered KYC action recommendations. That is to build an interconnected, technology-neutral national database system, associated with relevant civil registration and identity systems, and opened to authorized parties with the permission of customers. Authorized parties (like financial service providers) can gain access to the system reasonably and safely. Implement risk-based customer identification systems and verification requirements to facilitate access to low-risk digital financial services to achieve inclusive financial goals, like conducting a customer due diligence investigation layered framework that authorizes identification from one or more state verification sources.

3.3.2 Analysis framework of FSB financial technology

On March 16, 2016, the Financial Stability Board (FSB) held its 16th plenary session in Japan. For the first time, it officially discussed the systemic risks of financial technology and global regulatory issues. The conference report (Describing the Landscape and a Framework for Analysis Introduction) made a preliminary assessment of the micro and macro impacts of each major category of financial technology, and showed that there are indeed some potential regulatory concerns in terms of financial stability, which require regulators in various countries to cooperate and coordinate with each other. Therefore, the FSB requires various regulatory authorities not only to actively monitor the development of domestic financial technology, but also to cooperate with international organizations and institutions that formulate international rules in business monitoring, risk analysis and joint response.

Although global financial technology is still in its infancy and there are still specific obstacles such as insufficient data protection and too fast technology updates, the FSB focuses on financial stability. The proposed evaluation and analysis framework for financial technology is the overall supervision framework, which provides a useful reference for how regulatory authorities in various countries evaluate burgeoning financial technology. This framework is divided into three steps:

First, fully understand the innovative contents of various types of products of financial technology and characteristics of their institutions. It is necessary to recognize the essence of their business model: What are the main driving factors for service launch? Whether there are really demands for market in management and internal control or not requires analysis, especially the operation of the market road industry.

Second, distinguish between its driving factors and financial service innovation. The problems this step mainly solves are profiteering and money earned at an jaw-dropping speed in the name of innovation for innovative products and reducing costs, optimizing risk management, regulatory factors, and seriously inconsistent characteristics of the financial industry. Unmet market demand, macro technical factors, natural market evolution, emergence of new markets, economic integration factors, or other factors? For innovations that do help reduce costs, optimize risk management, fill gaps in financial services, and meet market demand, they should be supported on the basis of rectification and regulation. For violations of supervision or regulatory arbitrage, or even pseudo-innovation or criminal acts involving illegal fundraising, they should be severely cracked down on.

Third, it is necessary to pay attention to the impact of forward-looking assessments on financial stability, and fully evaluate it at the micro and macro levels. The micro level aims at analyzing the direct impact of innovation on financial markets and financial institutions. The issues needed to be addressed at the micro level include the followings. How does innovation affect the business models of traditional financial institutions? How will innovation change the behaviors of financial market entities and the overall market momentum? Towards where will the risk status of relevant financial institutions and other financial market entities evolve? How will the risk incentives faced by different institutions change? What vulnerability factors will innovation create at the institutional and market levels? Has the universal standard or target consensus related to the innovation been reached at the international level? Whether the innovation is subject to regulation, and to regulatory arbitrage or not is one of the factors that generate it. Specifically, which regulations provide this arbitrage space? At the micro level, the key assessment is made of the impact on the business model of traditional financial institutions, the mutual influence on the behaviors and risk conditions of participants in the financial market, and the vulnerability it may bring to the financial system. In other words, we should pay attention to the potential macro influences that may exist from the micro business model or products, which helps us to judge whether we should encourage or halt their business.

The macro level aims at understanding the impact of innovations on financial stability. The issues needed to be resolved at the macro level include the followings. Will this technological innovation bring systemically influential products or systems? Will it promote market fragmentation or centralization? Will there be a monopolistic industry structure? What kind of systemic impact will it have? How much complexity, transparency, liquidity, high leverage credit, and transaction opponents risks will it produce? How will it affect the system's term conversion, liquidity mismatch and risk change? What will happen to the market structure and market competition? What is the impact on crisis transmission channels? Has it changed or formed a network effect with positive externalities or negative externalities? Does it affect cross-border interconnections or systematically important institutional connections? Has a new systemically important association been created? Is it within the existing regulatory framework? Has financial business been moved beyond the scope of regulation? What are the vulnerability factors at the macro level? In other words, the macro level focuses on assessing whether financial technology activities will have a substantial impact on the complexity, transparency, liquidity, leverage, credit risk and transaction opponents risks of the financial system, on whether it will affect the entire system's term conversion, liquidity mismatch and risk change, and on whether they will have the substantial impact on market structure and competition, and the size of its externalities. The above areas are important aspects for comprehensively analyzing whether various types of financial technology activities will affect financial stability, and also for considering the future of various subdivision sectors.

The current financial technology is still in its infancy, and the evaluation of financial technology still has specific difficulties such as serious data shortages and high-speed technology updates. Therefore, it is no mean feat to answer all the questions raised in the above steps. The assessment framework proposed by the Financial Stability Board (FSB), however, has a clear layer, obvious focus, high feasibility, and strong practicality. And it is worthy for the regulatory authorities of various countries to learn from while dealing with the challenges of financial technology.

3.3.3 European Banking Authority (EBA)

1.The regulatory principles on financial technology

The European Banking Authority actively recognizes and will support the three major principles of financial technology supervision proposed by the European Commission: the principle of technology neutrality, the principle of appropriate supervision, and the principle of market integrity. Based on these, the European Banking Authority has put forward the principle of consumer protection. It believes that all regulatory authorities should follow this principle to reduce cyber security risks, prevent consumers' personal data and identity information from theft, and protect consumer rights.

2.Supervision of financial technology

EBA said that it was conducting a comprehensive review of financial technology companies in the EU at present, including their industry performance and their regulatory status under the EU and national regulatory frameworks. Preliminary observations showed that EU financial technology companies are subject to different levels of regulation and could be divided into three situations. They are supervised by EU financial regulations, or registered in accordance with national-level laws, or not subject to any EU or national-level regulations. Regulations at different levels may lead to problems such as regulatory arbitrage and fair competition. Whether from the perspective of prudential supervision or behavior supervision, different supervision ways for similar risks and products will be created by supervision with different scope and contents. The EBA noted that different regulatory methods used by various regulatory sectors to supervise financial technology regulatory arrangements such as regulatory sand boxes and innovation centers might cause problems of regulatory arbitrage and fair competition, posing risks to consumers and hindering financial stability. The EBA recommends that the EU amendments should include establishing regulatory principles. The financial technology processing principles of the same business, the same risks, and the same rules need to be clearly defined in the regulations, and to be reflected in various specific legislative amendments, and thus ensuring a fair competition environment for financial technology and preventing fragmented innovation policy and compromised market competition and regulatory arbitrage. In addition, anti-money laundering related laws and regulations need to be improved urgently, and care should be taken to prevent some countries from being too strict. On the one hand, the EU anti-money laundering and anti-terrorist financing framework was proposed in the EU Directive 2015/849 (the fourth anti-money laundering directive, 4AMLD), but the directive does not tell between financial technology and non-Fintech companies. As a result, it only applies to the so-called "obligation subject" as mentioned in Article 2 and enterprises that are required by member states to bear anti-money laundering and anti-terrorist financing responsibilities. On the other hand, the Fourth Anti-Money Laundering Directive demands few on the subject of obligations, while member states have the flexibility to formulate stricter standards when domestic legislation is in place. Therefore, overstrict laws and regulations in part of member states made it extremely difficult for customers to employ innovative solutions or financial technology solutions when conducting due diligence, hindering the development of financial technology companies. As a consequence, it is necessary to use financial investigation requirements in the process of conducting customer due diligence in order to achieve the obligation of the subject.

1.Regulatory intelligence on smart investment advisers

It is not necessary to formulate cross-industry regulations for the application of artificial intelligence in the financial industry. The report released at the end of 2016 stated that the risks of smart investment advisers in protecting consumer rights are mainly in the following areas.

First, consumers have limited access to information and the limited ability to process information. It may be unable to fully understand the financial advice provided by automated tools, or to fail to identify inappropriate advice and thus making wrong investment decisions.

Second, there might be something wrong with automated tools due to errors, hacking or malicious manipulation of algorithms, causing consumers to suffer losses.

Third, the unclear division of responsibilities leads to legal disputes.

Fourth, the same suggestions provided by various automated tools based on similar algorithms cause investors to adopt the same investment strategy for the same type of financial products, thus suffering losses.

In terms of the use of artificial intelligence in other areas of the financial industry, the joint report believes that the use of artificial intelligence in the financial industry is still in its early stages of development, and the degree of application in various fields is different. Currently, it is mainly focused on the field of investment consultants. It is , therefore, unnecessary to formulate cross-industry laws and regulations. Considering its development potential, however, EBA will continue to pay attention to the application of artificial intelligence in the banking industry. Next, for the big data analysis of financial consumers in the smart investment adviser, the joint report believes that its advantages lie in providing consumers with more personalized financial products, but the risks in consumer protection include the following.

First, personalized products reduce the comparability of consumers' choice of financial products, which is not conducive to making the best investment decisions.

Second, big data can be used to monitor and predict consumer preferences for specific products or institutions, thus providing targeted analysis and additional services, which may encourage consumers to make investment decisions that are not in their own interest.

Third, financial consumers may have difficulty in obtaining overall information about the degree of personalization of financial products and cannot fully understand it, which is not beneficial to the protection of consumers' rights and interests.

EU laws and regulations point out the main risks faced by financial consumers: First, consumers do not know or understand the use of personal data. Second, the consumers use their personal data improperly without consent. Third, financial institutions may refuse to transfer consumer personal data, leaving consumers with no freedom to choose other financial institutions. EBA's next steps in this area include the followings.

The first is the innovative use of consumer data by financial institutions. By soliciting opinions at the current stage, the final report will be issued within 2017.

Second, in view of the cross-industry nature of related risks, it will continue to cooperate with the European Securities and Insurance Regulatory Commission to carry out joint assessments, and raise specific issues such as price discrimination, financial exclusion, and credit ratings and non-transparency of decision-making. They will also be included in the joint assessment.

The third is to seek further policy measures, focusing on raising consumer awareness, strengthening regulatory coordination, encouraging cross-border exchanges and cooperation among relevant institutions in EU countries, ensuring that the implementation of the EU legal framework in each country is consistent, and improving legal certainty.

2.Supervision of cloud services

The EBA calls on the EU to develop and integrate regulatory rules for the use of cloud services by financial institutions as soon as possible. As a driving force for innovation, cloud services are increasingly important, and the banking industry is ever more interested in the use of cloud outsourcing solutions. In the United States, JPMorgan Chase Bank has used extensive public cloud services. EBA believes that it is necessary to provide specific guidance on cloud outsourcing, because cloud outsourcing has a high degree of regulatory uncertainty, which will hinder the use of cloud services by financial institutions. Different EU regulatory frameworks have different regulatory attitudes and approaches to cloud outsourcing, so coordination is needed. EBA recommends that the European Commission assess whether the current EU laws and regulations cover the risks associated with cloud outsourcing. In May 2017, EBA issued regulations and solicited opinions on the use of cloud services by the banking industry. On May 18, 2017, EBA released a recommendation draft on the use of outsourcing cloud services by credit institutions and investment companies. EBA hopes that the establishment of the above regulatory rules will provide regulatory guidance for banks and other financial institutions under their supervision to use cloud services. The draft proposes to unify the regulatory expectations and practices of cloud computing, and focuses on specifically ruling such five aspects as data and system security, data and data processing locations, access and audit authority, chain outsourcing, emergency planning and exit strategies. Considering the current industry giants that provide cloud services already have a certain say when negotiating contracts with financial institutions, the draft not only clarifies the regulatory expectations of the main contract clauses, but also expects specific regulatory rules to help financial institutions to better meet their own needs through negotiations and meet regulations.

3.Stance on supervision technology

EBA is also willing to join hands with various countries in the practice of supervision technology, cooperate with EU-level regulatory authorities, and cooperate with the industry, especially in the area of regulatory report, the enhancement of the effectiveness of supervision, and provide certain standard and compatible guarantees.

3.4 Financial technology regulation at the national level

National-level financial technology framework: Countries around the world have generally noticed the rapid development of financial technology in the market. In order to provide a good development environment for financial technology innovation in response to market changes, all countries have introduced measures against financial technology, including five aspects:

First is the introduction of the overall financial technology policy framework, such as the "Financial Technology Framework" introduced by the United States in early 2017; second is the establishment of financial technology regulatory arrangements that encourage innovation, such as the well-acclaimed "regulation sandbox"; third is the investigation of inappropriate laws and regulations. For example, South Korea and Japan relax financial regulations, and Australia strengthen retail payment regulations. The fourth is the provision of preferential policies such as taxes, guarantees and subsidies. Singapore's tax relief for financial technology startups, Israel's tax relief angel investment , and South Korea's secured loans are good cases in point. Fifth is new institutions within the regulatory department, such as internal financial technology departments and teams established by 12 supervision departments among 17 countries and regions surveyed, according to a report released by the International Securities Regulatory Commission in December 2016. In May 2017, the People's Bank of China also specially established the Financial Technology Committee, which focuses on the research, planning, and overall coordination of financial technology, and will actively develop and improve standards such as cloud computing, big data biometrics, and the trusted execution environment of mobile terminal PED.

3.4.1 Supervision arrangements of financial technology that encourages innovation at the national level

Many governments have actively promoted innovative financial technology regulatory arrangements, which can be broadly divided into three modelsie, Regulatory Sandbox, Innovation Hub, and Innovation Accelerator. Britain and leading countries in Singapore's financial technology regulation often combine three models.

1.Innovation hub

"Innovation center" model refers to supporting and guiding institutions (including regulated and unregulated institutions) to understand the financial regulatory framework and identify regulation, policy and legal issues in innovation. This model has been implemented in many countries and regions such as the United Kingdom, Singapore, Australia, Japan and Hong Kong, China. These include both one-on-one coaching support and support and guidance for wider audience. But this model does not involve real or virtual testing of innovative products and services. Given that this model is more operable, it seems that a large number of countries and regions will launch similar institutional arrangements in the future. Britain was the first country to launch this model. In October 2014, the UK's Financial Conduct Authority (FCA) launched a project called Project Innovate to help financial technology innovators become familiar with financial regulatory rules, understand whether they need to get business licenses from regulators, and how to obtain licenses. The main function of the project is consultation and suggestion, and it has obvious "informal" characteristics. The Innovation Hub team provides two types of consulting services during the establishment and operation of financial technology innovation companies: one is to provide policy advice and help startups obtain FCA licenses, like submitting business plans that comply with FCA regulations; the other is to provide supervision compliance consulting, including sending a team of experts to discuss innovative ideas and business opportunities with the company, helping companies understand their responsibilities, and discussing whether regulatory agencies need to revise laws and regulations. This model has an obvious "informal" feature, which is to make it clear that companies cannot rely on the contents of policy consultations, and FCA will not make policy commitments on the contents of consultations. This model can play a unique role in the early stages of the rise of financial technology. As the supervision sector, FCA has begun to stimulate the innovative dynamism of the market by the arrangement faced with the wave of financial technology innovation. It can also leave a very flexible participation space for the regulator itself. Based on this, it can know business models of financial technology, grasp the development trend of science and technology, and lay a solid foundation for the subsequent policy introduction. It is also of great significance for the enterprise. From the launch of the project in October 2014 to February 2016, a total of 413 requests for consulting (including 25 foreign companies' consulting requests) were received, of which 52% received consulting responses. Of these, 18 companies have already obtained licenses, and 21 companies are in the process of applying for licenses, and the other 48% of the cases are not supported, most because their conceptual ideas are relatively complete, and the licenses can be obtained directly through standard processes. Only few cases are not replied due to the FCA Innovation Center team's view that they are not in the interest of consumers.

2.Regulatory sandbox

The so-called "regulatory sandbox" model allows real or virtual testing of new financial technology products or services in a controllable test environment. This model simplifies market access standards and procedures within a limited scope, waives the application of some laws and regulations, and allows for the rapid implementation of new businesses on the premise of ensuring consumer rights, and can be promoted based on their testing in the sandbox. This model first appeared in Britain. After the British Financial Conduct Authority (FCA) launched an innovation project with policy consulting as its main function in 2014, it hopes to improve policy and processes and introduce more practical policy arrangements to encourage financial technology innovation. Therefore, FCA formally launched the Regulatory Sandbox project in May 2016 after brewing and soliciting opinions from the industry. Subsequently, Australia and Singapore released a project draft in June 2016. Singapore issued a regulatory sandbox guide in November the same year. In December 2016, Australia announced the policy details of the exemption of pilot financial technology companies' financial licenses. It is expected that similar arrangements will be launched by more countries and regions in the future. Judging from the existing British model and the Australian and New Zealand consultation draft, the regulatory sand boxes of different countries in the future will have characteristics in common in different specific arrangements. Whether the company is supervised by the regulated or unregulated institution, it will be included in the big pattern of supervision. For the first time, this initiative will make many financial technologies as "outsiders" reduce the risk of regulatory uncertainty in its innovative financial products. Regarding the current situation where countries mainly determine the scope of supervision through the institutional dimension, whether to cross the border is a supervision concept. How do you deal with the major challenges of the rapid development of financial technology? Second, applicants will receive personalized recommendations or guidance from the regulatory authorities on the innovative products or services they submit, which raises high demands on the regulatory authorities to understand and evaluate financial technology innovations. Third, some basic regulatory requirements, including consumer protection, will be set in the test environment. Fourth, during the testing process, supervisors still have supervisory tools and means that they can use. These last two points highlight the responsibilities that regulators still have in this sandbox for risk supervision and consumer protection.

The following takes the UK FCA Regulatory Sandbox for example to briefly introduce the operation of the Regulatory Sandbox.

The first is applicable standards. Five standards were raised by

FCA for Regulatory Sandbox to apply to innovative plans.

The first is whether it belongs to financial services.

The second is whether it is real innovation or not, which is a radical departure from existing products in the market.

The third is whether it can bring improved expectations for financial customers.

The fourth is whether it is tested by Regulatory Sandbox.

The fifth is whether innovation enterprises invest sufficient resources in the development of innovative approaches or not, and whether it knows applicable laws and regulations and it has taken measures to lower risks.

The second is the regulatory ways. Finally, FCA adopts two types of supervision methods for the projects in the sandbox. One is to issue restrictive licenses to innovative financial technology companies without financial licenses. Considering the failure of some innovative financial technology firms to obtain a financial business license and the lengthy application process for the related licenses, FCA will issue a restricted license called Restricted Authorization to them. Restricted licenses can be obtained in a shorter period of time, allowing companies to test their innovative solutions in a regulatory sandbox and ask the FCA to remove restrictions on their licenses after they are officially introduced to the market. The time needed at the process of applying for the removal of restrictions will be shorter than that for a complete financial license, which will reduce the administrative approval cost of the enterprise in general. The other is to innovate supervision methods for companies and outsourcing companies that already have financial licenses, including issuing a "No Enforcement Action Letter", "Individual Guidance" and using Waivers. The "No Enforcement Action Letter" means that the FCA takes "No Compulsory Measures" to the enterprise in the case that the innovation plan does not obviously violate the current PCA laws and regulations. "Individual Guidance" means that FCA lists the regulatory requirements to be applied to this innovative solution in an "individual" form. If the testing process does not violate the listed regulatory requirements, FCA will not take mandatory measures. The use of waivers means that the FCA can exercise the waivers within authority, allowing innovative solutions to be tested beyond current regulatory laws and regulations.

The third is consumer protection in a regulatory sandbox. In order to protect the rights of consumers, FCA mainly adopts the following four measures. The first is to limit the scope of consumers participating in the test. Consumers must know the content of the test, including the risks they face and the compensation they enjoy, so that companies can test their innovative products for consumers. The second is for FCA to decide the information disclosure, financial consumer rights protection and loss compensation scheme in the "supervised sandbox" test phase. The third is that consumers participating in the test enjoy all the statutory rights and benefits of ordinary financial consumers, such as the right to complain and the right to seek financial appeals (Financial Ombudsman Services, FOS), and the right of business to be compensated after the collapse under the Financial Compensation Scheme (FSCS). The fourth is to require the participating companies to have sufficient financial resources to compensate consumers for all their losses (including investment losses). In order to improve the effectiveness and flexibility of the regulatory sandbox, the FCA prefers to adopt the second method, which is to determine safeguards on an individual-case basis.

The fourth is the operation process of Regulatory Sandbox. According to the design of the FCA, innovative companies need to complete the regulatory sandbox test process through the following seven steps.

Step 1: The company submits an application for using the regulatory sandbox.

Step 2: The FCA evaluates whether it meets the requirements mentioned above.

Step 3: The FCA and the company jointly determine the regulatory sandbox plan, including the regulatory methods and consumer protection measures mentioned above.

Step 4: According to the determined regulatory methods, FCA adopts corresponding regulatory measures, like issuing restrictive licenses, or issuing No Enforcement Action Letter or Individual Guidance.

Step 5: The company starts testing based on the determined conditions.

Step 6: The company provides a test report to the FCA, and the FCA conducts a post-evaluation.

Step 7: After the FCA assessment, the enterprise can decide whether to bring the innovative solution to the market.

The whole process takes 3-6 months.

The Regulatory Sandbox model has five major advantages. To begin with, it reduces the time and cost for innovative businesses to enter the market. The uncertainty of the supervisor's attitude will hinder innovation. The FCA's estimate showed that regulatory uncertainty will delay the time to market for innovative businesses by one-third. The increased cost will reach 8% of the full income of the business throughout life cycle. The evaluation of the industry will be reduced by 15%, and the degree will increase. Obstacles emerged based on research from other industries. Disruptive innovation requires the growth stage of foreign financial companies and the support of external investment firms in the attitude of regulators, especially equity investments. Such uncertainties in innovative technologies will cause their valuations to decline, making it difficult for new products to enter the market. Many companies have no access to funding at all. Third, it can promote more ideas to be abandoned. Due to concerns of "Regulatory Sandbox" about the attitude of regulators, many innovative solutions can avoid the impact of regulatory uncertainty during the test phase without testing, thereby increasing the possibility that more innovative product businesses will eventually be traded. Fourth, it brings more types, lower costs and more convenient financial services to financial consumers. The regulatory sandbox contains a large amount of corporate data and true feedback from consumers. Start-ups can make full use of the market, industry and consumer conditions they reflect to improve innovative products and services. Fifth, during the regulatory sandbox testing process, supervisory authorities can take appropriate protective measures to forestall systemic risks. It is precisely because the "regulatory sandbox" is expected to achieve a good balance between encouraging innovation, controlling risks and protecting consumers that this model has been praised by all parties. Some countries or regional authorities have followed suit, making "Regulatory Sandbox" become a model for financial technology regulation.

Innovation accelerator model

"Innovation accelerator" model means that the regulators or government department establishes cooperation mechanisms with the industry to accelerate the development and application of financial technology innovation by providing financial support or policy support. The "incubator" arrangements in some countries also belong to this model. Given that regulators' responsibilities primarily focus on risk prevention and consumer protection, this model is expected to be adopted more by government agencies than by regulators. Generally speaking, the authorities of various countries currently hope to establish a good Fintech Ecosystem in their home countries, and establish and cultivate a financial technology industry through communication and cooperation between the government, regulatory authorities, traditional financial institutions, and financial technology industries. They also expect the ecosystem to stimulate technological innovation, attract financial technology talents, improve the efficiency of financial markets and the financial system, and enhance the satisfaction experience of financial consumers. Establishing a Fintech ecosystem includes four key success factors.

The first is the business environment. That is the Fintech ecosystem must create an overall cost advantage, have the advantages of financial and technological talents, form an institution and talent pool, integrate various service resources, and have high-quality and low-cost infrastructure. The second is government support. The government influences the ecosystem at many levels. In Europe and the United States where Fintech development is relatively mature, the government focuses on the establishment of laws and regulations to guide the development of the industry. In other regions, such as Singapore, the government is more involved in the entire ecosystem, plans industrial development policies, optimizes the business environment, provides tax incentives, and relaxes investment incentives such as foreign talent introduction. The third is capital acquisition and market investment, which is the decisive force, but the government can provide innovative business development funds, and introduce private funds, venture capital, financial institutions and other related funds to help raise funds and provide initial financial support. The government can also independently or cooperate with other institutions to set up innovation accelerators, provide operating facilities, and alleviate capital pressure on new entrepreneurs.

The fourth is counselling and consulting. The government can help Fintech start-ups to complete their establishment and development processes through innovation centers or accelerators starting from the optimization of business models, to the application for the required licenses, and to the compliance operation at the later stages. In the establishment of a good Fintech ecosystem, policy guidance is used to encourage various strategic cooperation and integration between large financial institutions and Fintech companies, which is an important means to promote the rapid integration of finance and technology. At present, various large financial institutions and some exchanges in the world are rapidly carrying out various co-operations with Fintech companies, like financial institutions purchasing Fintech companies' core technologies or business models, cooperating through shareholding, and outsourcing some of the business to Fintech companies. It is foreseeable that the development of Fintech in various countries depends, to a large extent, on the close cooperation between traditional financial institutions and Fintech companies. In addition, since a large part of Fintech's service targets are groups that are not served by the traditional financial system, such customers have less financial expertise and lower risk tolerance. Regulatory authorities in various countries have placed consumer protection in more prominent position. It mainly includes three aspects: The first is to strengthen information disclosure and fully fulfill the obligation of risk notification. For example, the "Regulatory Methods on Internet Crowdfunding and Issuance of Non-Realizable Securities Through Other Media" issued by the FCA in the UK requires that P2P platforms should use popular language to accurately disclose investment product returns and risks to investors. The Participatory Financing Act issued by France in 2014 requires that equity crowd funding platforms must set up a "step-by-step access procedure". The first step is to in-form investors of the nature of the investment and its risks. The second step is to test the appropriateness of the investor before the investor subscribes, including the investors experience, knowledge, family and inheritance, and enable the investors to confirm the compatibility of the project with its own capabilities. The second is to improve the Internet financial consumer complaint handling mechanism. For example, the SEC supervises the P2P platform in the United States, the Consumer Financial Protection Bureau (CFPB) is responsible for collecting data on P2P lending finance consumers complaints, and the Federal Trade Commission (FTC) is responsible for monitoring and stopping the unfair and fraudulent behaviors of P2P platforms, and has law enforcement responsibility for consumer complaints about P2P lending. The third is to strengthen consumer information protection and formulate corresponding punishment measures. Regulators in Britain and the United States have required Fintech companies to publish consumer privacy protection systems and have drew up corresponding penalties for violations.

3.5 Development and outlook of financial technology

3.5.1 Professional supervision technology startups

Although the term supervision technology has only been proposed for a year or two, a large number of supervision technology startups have emerged over the past five years, each focusing on a particular area of compliance. At present, there are no recognized top start-ups, and some companies have higher media exposure. Some companies have higher financing amounts, like Onfido (identity management with a financing of 30 million US dollars), and some companies have received valuable industry concerns such as Ayasdi (risk modeling and was deeply involved in Citi's stress tests), Sybenetix (behavioral analysis in a transaction environment), and Suade (oversight as a service overall platform founded by former bankers Barclays and Mizuho). Some research institutions have listed 21 supervision technology start-ups most worth paying attention to in Europe and the United States, including Trulioo which specializes in identification recognition, KYC Exchange and Trunomi which provide auxiliary KYC services, and other startups with anti-fraud and risk monitoring as the main focus.

3.5.2 Cooperation between traditional financial or technology companies and supervision technology startups

Take the cooperation between Simmons & Simmons in the UK and the start-up Suade, and the cooperation between regulatory reporting software provider Abide Financial and the European financial transaction information database REGIS-TR for example.

Large financial or technological companies invest in the field of supervision technology. With deep industry knowledge and strong development capabilities, large institutions are expected to make the most competitive progress in this area. Bloomberg, for example, has introduced a transaction cost analysis (TAC) system that helps organizations meet EU MIFIDII requirements. Switzerland's SIX Group and Nasdaq are at the same time launching related products or services for transaction monitoring and data security. Among them, IBM's acquisition of Promontory is a milestone. On September 29, 2016, IBM announced that it plans to acquire U.S. compliance consultation company Promontory. It has over 600 former experts in banking and regulatory fields. Promontory was expected to teach Watson compliance and risk control expertise to oversee technology at Watson, the top cognition calculation analysis technology platform. IBM will use the acquisition to create a new subsidiary, Watson Financial Services, and develop cognitive tools for compliance tracking, financial risk modeling, and anti-money laundering monitoring systems. This case was significant in supervision technology industry, marking that supervision technology, a field at the early stages of development and acquisition, has acquired important commercial recognition and development potential.

In terms of market size, the global demand for regulation, compliance and governance software was expected to have reached $118.7 billion by 2020. In the next five years, North America will surpass Europe and Ten Asia Countries to become the country with the largest spending on regulatory software. Currently, 35% of supervision software is spent in the Asia Pacific. In Europe, the agency predicts that the UK supervision technology will reach 15 billion pounds in market size per year, which is about 0.7% of UK GDP. RegTech, the supervision technology, not only serves traditional financial institutions, but also provides compliance services for emerging Fintech companies, which is a very important potential market. It is urgent to improve their compliance and risk control capabilities and levels because many Fintech companies have entered the financial industry as outsiders.

3.6 The future of financial technology supervision

Globally, the positive role of regulatory rule of law in financial technology is prominent. Considering the development trend of financial technology in various countries, the development of financial technology is relatively stable in countries with good supervision and the spirit of rule of law. However, if there are no regulatory arrangements at the beginning, or if they are not included in the existing regulatory principles, coupled with the lack of practitioners' spirit of rule of law, problems may emerge. In some places, issues such as anti-terrorism sole financing, anti-money laundering, and consumer protection may arise.

There are two problems with regulation on financial technology globally.

First, the regulatory measures vary from country to country, and there is no global uniform standard. Regarding the specific supervision of various types of financial technology, due to the different innovation and maturity levels of various financial technologies, currently countries are mainly considering and implementing the supervision of network financing and electronic money. In other financial technology categories, the regulatory rules for payments in various countries are relatively mature, while technologies such as blockchain and its impact is still in the exploratory stage. In general, there are large differences in the supervision of specific financial technology categories in various countries. The global regulation of financial technology lacks unified standards and is fragmented.

The second is the insufficient regulatory cooperation because of the financial technology cross-border exhibition industry. At present, the traditional financial industry has begun to gradually accept the borderless competition of the financial technology industry. But the cross-border regulatory cooperation arrangements for financial technology have clearly lagged behind cross-border exhibition industry. Take Ant Financial for example. Its internationalization is accelerating, payments have covered more than 220 countries and regions, and serves over 300,000 overseas customers a year. Meanwhile, it has invested in companies in India. The joint venture Internet banks in South Korea has been approved for construction. It plans to build banks or payment institutions in some Southeast Asian countries. European cross-border P2P business is also a typical example. For traditional commercial banks, there are already a series of institutional arrangements for cooperation between the supervisory authorities of the home country and the host country, including communication and cooperation between the supervisory authorities of the home country and the host country in terms of information sharing, cross-border inspection, continuous coordination, and disposal plan. However, there are currently no institutional arrangements for the financial technology companies that have launched cross-border operations, in terms of regulation or consumer protection. Considering the cross-border exhibition industry of financial technology is still in its infancy, the regulatory cooperation problems currently encountered are mainly concentrated in the field of market access. Financial technology companies have no arrangement for joint assessment of possible systematic importance in the future. At present, there are already huge financial technology companies, and some companies are also expanding globally. If they continue their current development momentum, they will inevitably need to conduct a joint assessment of global "systemic importance" financial technology in the future, and appropriately respond in a corresponding supervision based on the assessment.

Based on the above issues and combined with the current situations of financial technology supervision at the national and international levels discussed above, we believe that in the future financial technology will certainly be included in a larger scope within the framework of prudential regulation, behavior regulation and macro-prudential regulation.

At the national level, the scope of regulatory responsibilities is clarified and the existing regulatory framework is included. Regardless of how financial technology is defined, it is an international consensus to supervise financial activities based on the nature of the business. Most countries and regions require that financial technology innovations must follow existing basic principles of financial regulation to ensure consistency in standards. So, is it necessary to set up a new institution to supervise financial technology? Whether at the international or the national level, it is generally believed that no new institution is needed. The supervision of financial technology can continue to use the existing supervision structure, and the existing supervision department shall perform the supervision duties according to the institution or function. But a very important point is that at the initial stage of financial technology development, a very clear border of regulatory responsibilities is required. It is not easy for developing countries or developed countries. How do we accurately classify financial technology? Whether to supervise the equity and debt financing in different ways? How we decide must be different, the core lies in clarifying the responsibilities within the existing regulatory framework.

The U.S. Office of the Comptroller of the Currency (OCC) announced in December 2016 that it was considering the issuance of special bank licenses to financial technology for a special purpose, which is a good example of this trend. On December 2, 2016, OCC issued a consultation titled "Exploring the Issuance of Special Purpose National Bank Charters for Fintech Companies", which describes legal authority and necessary conditions for OCC to issue special purpose licenses. The report clearly stated that if a Fintech company obtains a national banking license, it must meet the same high standards in security, reliability, fair access, and fair treatment of consumers as all federally licensed agencies. The deadline for feedback is January 15, 2017. According to the current public feedback, although some state regulators such as the New York State Financial Services Authority have objections to this plan, the market generally welcomes this move by OCC. At the international level, international governance is accelerating and bilateral cooperation has gradually begun. After the Financial Stability Board formally included Fintech in its agenda in March 2016, its industry committees such as bank, securities and insurance have accelerated their work in this area. The regulatory framework has begun to take shape, and more detailed regulatory standards are being studied at the working group level. In the next year or two, it is expected that international regulatory committees such as the Basel Committee on Banking Supervision (BCBS), the International Organization of Securities Commission (IOSCO), and the Association of Bank Insurance Supervisors (IANS) will issue further Fintech assessment reports. With the development of financial technology and the current international regulatory framework, content that does not adapt to market development needs to be revised. Is it necessary to change the content of the new action plan? Under the international governance and content supervision cooperation model, the key members' associations will make professional and authoritative judgments.

The Second Part

Technology

Chapter 4 Blockchain Technology

4.1 Origin

The blockchain is derived from the network technology Point to Point. In P2P, the files to be downloaded are divided into countless pieces, which are expanded to different computers. These computers can download some, and at the same time transfer the obtained pieces to each other. In the end, they can be combined into a complete file as required. Network video companies were the first to use P2P technology, so they were also the earliest industries interested in blockchain technology. P2P technology makes point-to-point computing, storage and transmission between many computers possible, opening up the possibility of distributed storage.

Just as the computers on the network jointly maintain the integrity of a video file, when people conduct transactions through the network, the entire transaction process of a digital asset will be recorded on the "ledger", which is jointly maintained by the computers on the network and is not in the hands of an institution or individual called a distributed ledger. To quote what R3's CTO Brown (Richard G. Brown) said, "When a batch of entries is added to the ledger, the index number of the previous batch is also added, so that all participants can verify the source of all entries on the ledger. These are called 'blocks', and all the blocks together are called the blockchain."

P2P has been criticized for being widely used in the download and distribution of pirated music, film and television. The blockchain is also the basic technology of Bitcoin. Blockchain technology is in line with the trends of open source and distributed Internet and software technology. The sharing, efficiency, democratization, decentralization, and transparent trust brought by these technologies have broad application prospects after the popularity of the Internet.

4.2 Definition

Blockchain refers to the technical solution of collectively maintaining a reliable database through "decentralization" and "detrust". (Integrate mathematics, finance, law and information technology). The core of the blockchain is to solve trust and security issues. Blockchain is a trust relationship that is free from personality and is established by code, agreement, and rules.

4.2.1 Four technical innovation

The first is called a distributed ledger. The transaction records are jointly completed by multiple nodes distributed in different places. Each node records a complete account. Therefore, they can participate in monitoring the legality of transactions and can also jointly testify for it . Unlike traditional centralized bookkeeping schemes, no one node can record accounts individually, thereby eliminating the possibility of a single bookkeeper being controlled or bribed to keep false accounts. There being enough accounting nodes, in theory, unless all nodes are destroyed, the accounts will not be lost, thereby ensuring the security of the account data.

Distributed ledger technology can also be used to clearly define and protect property rights, such as digital currency, real estate transactions, securities transactions and other areas where ownership changes frequently. For example, for those works that are widely spread on the Internet, the rights of the creators can be protected using blockchain technology. The effective combination of law and code can address the inherent requirements of economic life such as the rule of law, supervision, rights, efficiency, and integrity.

The second is called symmetric encryption and authorization technology. The transaction information stored on the blockchain is public, but the account identity information is highly encrypted and can only be accessed with the authorization of the data owner, thereby ensuring the data's security and personal privacy.

The third is called the consensus mechanism, which is to reach consensus among all bookkeeping nodes to determine the validity of a record. This is both a means of identification and a means of preventing tampering. The blockchain proposes four different consensus mechanisms that are suitable for different application scenarios which strikes a balance between efficiency and security. Take Bitcoin for example. A proof of workload is used. Only when more than 51% of the accounting nodes in the entire network are controlled, it is possible to forge a record that does not exist. When there are enough nodes added to the blockchain, this is basically impossible, thereby eliminating the possibility of counterfeiting.

The fourth technical feature is called smart contracts which are based on these credible, and non-tamperable data, to automatically execute some pre-defined rules and terms. Take insurance for example. If personal medical information and risk information are authentic, then it is easy to automate claims in some standardized insurance products.

In short, blockchain technology is a new type of information technology required by Internet finance. It can use IT technology to solve many urgent problems in the financial industry.

We can describe blockchain technology as follows. Blockchain is a science that integrates disciplines such as mathematics, finance, law, and information technology to solve the problem of trust between people.

Blockchain is a technology generated after the development of information technology to a certain degree, which uses a concept of "information redundancy", "high-speed transmission", and "distributed" to produce a data storage mechanism that is difficult to be destroyed and that has mutual trust and cooperation between groups.

4.3 Characteristics of blockchain technology

1.Decentralization

Due to the use of distributed accounting and storage, there is no centralized hardware or management organization, and the rights and obligations of any node are equal. The data blocks in the system are jointly maintained by the nodes with maintenance functions in the entire system and adopt pure mathematics method in place of the original central organization, and the trust relationship between nodes is stronger.

The blockchain system is built on the basis of networks, with equal rights, open data, distributed data, and highly redundant storage that cannot be tampered with.

The blockchain system is based on the consensus system, which is programmable, intelligent, confidential, and personalized.

2.Open and transparent

The blockchain system is open. Except for the private information of the parties to the transaction, the blockchain data is open to everyone. Anyone can check the blockchain data and develop related applications through the open interface. Information, therefore, is highly transparent.

3.Autonomy

The blockchain uses consensus-based regulations and protocols (such as a set of open and transparent algorithms) to enable all nodes in the entire system to exchange data freely and securely in a detrusted environment, so that the trust in "people" is changed to the trust in machine, causing no human intervention will work. There is no need to trust each other between the nodes that participate in data exchange in the entire system. The operating rules of the entire system are open and transparent, and all data content is also public. Therefore, within the scope of the rules and time specified by the system, They cannot cheat each other.

4.Collective maintenance

All nodes in the distributed system can participate in the verification process of the data block (such as Bitcoin "mining"), and each node shares rights and obligations.

5.Unchangeable information

Once the information is verified and added to the blockchain, it will be permanently stored. Unless more than 51% of the nodes in the system can be controlled at the same time, the modification of the database on a single node is invalid, so the data of the blockchain is stable and its reliability is high.

The security of the blockchain system is guaranteed by the powerful computing power formed through mining. Because each transaction is sequentially linked by time-stamping, when a person wants to forge a transaction, he not only needs to forge the block corresponding to the transaction, but also needs to forge the link method behind it. Blocks go successively very fast, because many people share the blockchain. If the computing power of the forger's computer cannot exceed the forged area, it will be found and removed immediately.

6. Reliable datebase

The entire system will be in the form of a sub-database so that each participating node can obtain a copy of the complete database.

Unless more than 51% of the nodes in the entire system can be controlled at the same time, modifications to the database on a single node are invalid and cannot affect the data content on other nodes. Therefore, the more nodes participating in the system and the stronger the computing power, the higher the data security in the system.

7. Anonymity

The rules will judge whether the activity is valid by themselves. Because the exchange between nodes follows a fixed algorithm, its data interaction is not trusted. The program trust in the blockchain is very helpful for the accumulation of credit. Therefore, the transaction side does not need to make the other one produce concepts that there is no trust between nodes by means of make identity public. There is, therefore, no need for nodes to disclose their identity. Each participating node in the system is anonymous.

8. Open source

Since the operating rules of the entire system must be open and transparent, the entire system must be open-source for the program. Everyone can take part for free to jointly promote the development and progress of blockchain technology.

9. Cross-border

At present, cross-border remittances go through layers of foreign exchange control agencies, and transaction records are recorded by multiple parties. However, if you are making transaction with Bitcoin, a large amount of funds will pass by entering the digital address directly, click the mouse, and wait for P2P to confirm the transaction. No cross-border transaction record will be left without going through any regulatory agency.

10.Knockoff is hard to survive

Since the blockchain technology algorithm is completely open-source, anyone can download the source code, modify some parameters, and recompile it to create a new blockchain. However, creating these copycat versions requires controlling 51% of the computing power of the genuine one, but the number of hosts required will be an astronomical figure if doing so. The price is too high to pay so it is difficult for the knockoff to survive.

4.4 Blockchain technology foundation

4.4.1 Basic structure: It consists of blocks, which form a chain structure by orderly connection

Block: A record in the blockchain that contains related transaction information.

Mining refers to the formation of new blocks through calculation, which is a process in which transaction supporters use their computer hardware to perform mathematical calculations for the network to confirm transactions and improve security. Take Bitcoin for example. Transaction supporters (miners) run Bitcoin software on their computers to constantly calculate the cryptographic issues provided by the software to ensure transactions. As a reward for the service, miners can get the fees included in the transactions they confirmed and the newly created Bitcoin.

Hash: Hash, generally translated as "sanlie", but also directly transliterated as "haxi", that is, input of arbitrary length (also known as pre-image), through the hash algorithm, is transformed into a fixed-length output, which is the hash value. This conversion is a kind of compression reflection whose space of the hash value is usually much smaller than that of the input . Different input may hash into the same output, so it is impossible to uniquely determine the input from the hash value. To put it simply, it is a function that compresses messages of any length to a certain-length message digest.

The nature of Hash

All hash functions have the following basic characteristics: If the two hash values are different (based on the same function), the original input of the two hash values is also different, which is a result of why the hash function is determined. On the other hand, the input and output of the hash function are not corresponding. If the two hash values are the same, the two input values are likely to be the same, but the two must be equal, we cant say. Input some data to calculate the hash value, and then partially change the input value. A hash function with strong confusion characteristics will produce a completely different hash value.

Typical hash functions have infinite domains of definition, such as byte strings of any length, and limited value domains, such as fixed-length bit strings. In some cases, the hash function can be designed to have domains of definition and ranges of the same size. Corresponding hash functions are also called permutations. Reversibility can be achieved by using a series of reversible “mixing” operations on input values.

Hash application example: SHA256, an encryption algorithm for hash value How SHA256 works: enter any string of data into SHA256, and you will get a 256-digit hash value. Its characteristic is that the same data input will get the same results. As long as the input data changes slightly (for example, a 1 becomes 0), a very different result will be obtained, which cannot, however, be predicted in advance. Forward calculation (calculating the corresponding hash value based on the data) is very easy. Reverse calculation (commonly known as "decipher", that is, calculating its corresponding data based on the hash value) is extremely difficult and is considered impossible under the current technological conditions.

Digital signature: it involves a hash function, the sender's public, and private key, with two functions: one is to determine that the message is indeed signed and sent by the sender; the other is that the digital signature can determine the integrity of the message. The digital signature works as follows: When sending a message, the sender uses a hash function to generate a message digest from the message text, and then uses its own private key to encrypt the digest. The encrypted digest will be used as the digital signature of the message to be sent to the receiver. The receiver first uses the same hash function as the sender to calculate the message digest from the received original message, and then uses the public key of the sender to encrypt the additional digital signature. If the two digests are the same, then the receiver can confirm that the digital signature belongs to the sender.

Time-stamp: It is used for comparison and verification processing. The time-stamp server is a time authority system based on PKI (Public Key Infrastructure) technology, which provides accurate and reliable time services. It uses a safety mechanism that determines the strength criteria with precise time to confirm the existence of the system processor at a certain time and the relative chronological order of related operations, providing basic services for time anti-repudiation in information systems.

Working process: new transaction requirements are broadcast to all nodes each node collects the requirements into a block each node generates a random string and calculates each node gets an answer that matches the random number and broadcast to all nodes the node verifies the transaction. After the node is valid, all nodes accept the block the node starts to create a new block and adds the data just now.

4.4.2 Bitcoin transaction process

Bitcoin transaction certification mechanism

The Bitcoin transaction certification mechanism currently falls into two categories: pos (proof of stake) rights and interests certification mechanism and pow (proof of work) workload certification mechanism.

The proof of work mechanism is to get rewards based on how much work is done, whose disadvantage is that the computing power is easily centralized.

(2)Bitcoin credit system establishment process

In order for the entire network to recognize the validity of each transaction, it must be broadcast to each node (miner).

Each miner node must time-stamp each transaction lasting 10 minutes and record it in that block.

Each node has to compete for the legal bookkeeping right of this 10-minute block by solving the SHA256 puzzle, and strives to get a reward of 25 Bitcoins (during the first 4 years, you will get 50 Bitcoins every 10 minutes, which is halved every 4 years) .

If a node succeeded in solving the 10-minute SHA256 problem, he will publish all time-stamped transactions recorded in his 10-minute block to the entire network, which will be verified by other nodes across the network.

Other nodes on the entire network check the correctness of the bookkeeping in the block. Without errors, they will compete for the next block after the legal block, thus forming a single chain of legal bookkeeping blocks, that is, the general ledger of the Bitcoin payment system-the blockchain.

Generally speaking, each transaction must not be accepted as a legal transaction on the final blockchain until 6 block confirmations, that is, 6 10-minute sinks.

The so-called "Bitcoin" is such a billing system: it includes the owner using a private steel to electronically sign and pay to the next owner, and then the entire network of "miners" covers the time and records, forming a blockchain and making transactions.

(3)Working steps of blockchain formation

New transaction requirements are broadcast to all nodes.

Each node collects new transaction requirements into a block.

Each node starts to generate random strings continuously, and calculates random number answers.

When a node's answer matches a random number, it broadcasts the generated block to all nodes.

The node verifies the transaction. When the transaction contained in the block is valid, all nodes accept the block.

The node starts to create new blocks and adds the hash of the newly-accepted block.

(4)Consensus agreement

Each full node independently verifies each transaction according to comprehensive standards.

By completing the verification of the proof-of-work algorithm, mining nodes independently package transaction records into new blocks, and each node independently verifies the new blocks and assembles them into the blockchain. Each node independently selects the blockchain and chooses the longest blockchain under the proof-of-work mechanism.

4.4.3.Block formation process

After the current block is added to the blockchain, all miners immediately begin the generation of the next block:

Record transaction information in local memory into the block body

Generate a Merkle tree of all transaction information in the block body, and save the value of the Merkle tree root in the block head;

Use the SHA256 algorithm to generate a hash value from the block header data of the last block just produced, and fill it into the hash value of the current block

Save current time in time-stamp field

The difficulty value field will be adjusted according to the average generation time of the block in the previous period to respond to the ever-changing total calculation amount of the entire network. If it increases, the system will increase the difficulty of the math problem so that the time expected to complete next block is still within a certain time.

4.4.4 Multiprocessing resolution mechanism

Forking mechanism

Meanwhile, more than one node in the entire network can calculate a random number, that is, there will be multiple nodes in the network broadcasting their respective temporary blocks (all are legal). If a node receives multiple subsequent temporary blocks for the same predecessor block, the node will establish a branch on the local blockchain, and multiple temporary blocks correspond to multiple branches. This deadlock will be broken until the next proof of work is found, among which, one chain is confirmed to be a longer one. The nodes that work on the other branch chain will change camps and start to work on the longer chain. The other branches will be completely abandoned by the network.

4.4.5 The solution: double payment

Double payments refer to attackers use the same money for different transactions almost simultaneously.

Whenever a node adds a newly received transaction ticket to the block, it will check whether the currency used in the current transaction actually belongs to the current transaction initiator along with the public key, which can cover the original birth point of the coin (that is, the source of the block that produced it). Although multiple transaction orders can be broadcast in any order, they must be presented in a certain order when they are eventually added to the block. The blocks are chronological by time stamp, which determines that the source of any transaction funds can be definitely traced back.

4.5 Blockchain platform

The blockchain platform is divided into a basic framework layer (Basic Chain) and an application adaptation layer (Application adapter). The former is based on the basic protocol cluster, including basic modules such as currency protocols, account protocols, ledger protocols, consensus protocols, and P2P networking protocols. Different applications can be equipped with different basic protocol modules. The application adaptation layer provides the functional components (assets, transactions, and contracts) required by applications at the upper level; provides the private key storage and management required by the account system; provides the visual tools required by operation and maintenance management (configuration, monitoring, data analysis and blockchain browser).

4.6 Blockchain network architecture

Blockchain currently falls into three categories, of which hybrid blockchains and private blockchains can be considered broadly defined private chains.

4.6.1 Public blockchain

Public blockchain refers to the fact that any individual or group in the world can send transactions, which can obtain valid confirmations of the blockchain, and anyone can participate in its consensus process. The common blockchain is the earliest blockchain, and is, at present, the most widely used blockchain. The virtual digital currencies of the Bitcoin series belong to the public blockchain, and there is only one blockchain in the world corresponding to this currency.

4.6.2 Consortium blockchain

A number of pre-selected nodes are designated as bookkeepers within a group, and the generation of each block is jointly determined by all pre-selected nodes (they participate in the consensus process). Other access nodes can participate in the transaction, but don't ask about the bookkeeping process. (In essence, it is still managed accounting, and it just becomes distributed accounting. The number of pre-selected nodes and how to determine the bookkeeper of each block becomes the main risk point of the blockchain), anyone else can conduct qualified inspection through API opened by blockchain.

4.6.3 Private blockchain

The private blockchain only uses the general ledger technology of the blockchain for bookkeeping. It can be a company or an individual, and enjoys the permission of the blockchain, no different from other distributed stored methods.

4.7 Evolution of blockchain

The essence of blockchain technology is a distributed authentication protocol. In the development process of blockchain technology, the gradual evolution has gone through the following stages.

Blockchain1.0: Digital currency. The first software implementation of blockchain technology is Bitcoin, which means that Blockchain1.0 implements digital electronic currency functions, which is the early stage of blockchain technology.

Blockchain2.0: digital assets and smart contracts. At this stage, blockchain technology is gradually recognized by everyone, and various applications are rapidly developing, gradually replacing traditional methods in the fields of digital assets and smart contracts. Therefore, Blockchain2.0 is, in essence, an ownership registration and authentication system, which is committed to realizing market transactions and commercial credit behaviors, including bonds, insurance, foreign exchange, stocks, futures, options and other financial activities and the occasion where credit reporting and smart contracts are required such as leases, crowdfunding, and the Internet of Credit. Software which can be referred to are, for example, Ethereum.

Blockchain 3.0: DAO, DAC (Blockchain Autonomous Organization, Blockchain Autonomous Company)-big blockchain society (science, medicine, and education, along with blockchain + artificial intelligence).

Blockchain 3.0 is to write the unified language of human beings, economic behavior, social system and even life into a basic software protocol. The unified language integrates the natural language of all human races into a low-entropy expression and provides an interface with computer languages; human economic behavior, social institutional systems, and life regeneration mechanisms are collectively referred to as the time currency system. Blockchain3.0 is a distributed artificial intelligence operating system that integrates a unified language and time currency.

Blockchain3. 0 is a networked computer-assisted artificial intelligence operating system, with the intention of achieving self-organizing institutions, distributed node mutual trust social networks, the corresponding economic and social systems, and even a decentralized government.

Blockchain is a basic software protocol that can evolved into an self-organizational structure. Self-organization is a concept of complexity. The content of complexity includes non-linear theory, chaos and fractal, new and old theories (dissipation theory, synergy theory, catastrophe theory, information theory, cybernetics and system theory), and its characteristics are power law, small world, and are scale-free.

The current blockchain technology is mainly based on blockchain1. 0 and blockchain2.0.

Application of blockchain technology

First, blockchain is a technology, not a product. It develops with the existing technology products, rather than subverting the current world order.

The main advantages of blockchain are that it does not require the participation of intermediaries, the process is efficient and transparent, the cost is low, and the data is highly secure. So an industry with requirements for any of this will have opportunities to use blockchain technology.

For example, due to the prevention of single points of failure and systemic risks in the financial industry, layer-by-layer audits are required to control financial risks, but high internal cost is brought about. Blockchain technology can greatly reduce costs for the entire financial system through tamper-resistant and highly transparent methods.

The open and immutable characteristics of the blockchain make its application reach far beyond the field of accounting, providing various types of records management applications, such as supply chain management, company management processes, government department data management, audit systems, property deeds, and land property records, which can improve the operational efficiency of the organization.

Bitcoin can be regarded as the first practical application that is generated simultaneously with the blockchain. In addition to virtual currencies, blockchain technology can be applied to many industries and fields.

The blockchain concept can be applied to real estate property insurance, sharing economy, electricity, banking, payment, stock equity, legal data, transactions, money laundering prevention, internet of things, music, copyright, proof of equity, privacy data, auditing systems, government credit and authentication system.

4.8.1 Bitcoin-blockchain technology

In 2019, Satoshi Nakamoto developed the operating system for coin issuance, transaction and account management on P2P (peer-to-peer) networks and distributed database platforms based on the concepts of openness, reciprocity, consensus, and direct participation, combined with the work model of kaihengmujian and block ciphers in cryptography.

Its system allows every node throughout the peer-to-peer network user terminal to reach a network agreement in accordance with its seed file, thereby ensuring fairness, security, and reliability in currency issuance, management, and circulation. It promises that Bitcoin will become an "e-cash" similar to email, and uses a cryptographic design to ensure the security of all aspects of currency circulation. Since then, its peer-to-peer network and its first blockchain have begun operation, and has issued 50 Bitcoins ever.

In online payments, cash is converted into numbers, and there are two risks:

(1) Numbers (or currencies) are easy to be changed, which are prone to produce counterfeit illegal currency.

(2) The numbers are easy to copy, which may cause a person to pay twice with the same money.

In the process of online payment, a third-party supervisory institution must be required to ensure the security and reliability of payment. We transfer money from one account to another one by electronic banks, and all are performed by banks (and bank transaction agencies) transaction system. The currency has never been stored on our computer. Instead, it is stored in the bank's database. A bank is a centralized transaction supervisor.

(trust basedmodel):

Satoshi Nakamoto believes that third-party processing of electronic payment information is inherently subject to the weakness of the "trust based model": people cannot achieve completely irreversible transactions because financial institutions always inevitably come forward to resolve disputes. In turn, the existence of financial intermediaries will increase the cost of transactions, limit the practical minimum transaction size, and confine daily small-amount payment transactions.

Many goods and services are not returned by themselves. Without irreversible payment methods, Internet trade will be greatly restricted. Due to the potential for a refund, the trust of both parties to the transaction is required. Because merchants must also be careful of their customers, they will ask customers for completely unnecessary personal information. In actual business behavior, a certain percentage of fraudulent customers are also considered unavoidable, and related losses are treated as sales expenses.

Satoshi Nakamoto, therefore, believes that we need such an electronic payment system, which is based on cryptographic principles rather than credit, so that any two parties reaching consensus can directly make payment without the participation of a third-party intermediary. Eliminating the possibility of reverse payment transactions can protect specific sellers from fraud; and for those who want to protect buyers, setting up a usual third-party guarantee mechanism in this environment is also easy and pleasant .

In Satoshi Nakamoto's thesis, he proposed a kind of electronic transaction certificate that are arranged and recorded in chronological order by point-to-point distributed time stamp server, so as to solve the problem of double payment. As long as the total sum of computing power controlled by honest nodes is greater than that of computing power of cooperative attackers, the system is secure.

Differences from traditional electronic money: Bitcoin is decentralized, the stock is limited, the code is open, and the value comes from the increase in customers.

Bitcoin is decentralized, while traditional electronic money has a central service provider, which makes the system of Bitcoin without a separate loophole relatively stable.

Bitcoin's account is anonymous, but because the transaction history is completely public, coupled with sufficient human resources and time, the account can be traced back to real-name users, in principle, through the transaction chain.

Bitcoin's stock is limited and cannot be issued at will, while traditional electronic money can be issued indefinitely. This characteristic makes Bitcoin's holding value higher.

Bitcoin's code is open, while that of traditional electronic money is closed. Merchants, consumers, investors, and service providers can create a very rich service and financial system around this open source system.

The value of Bitcoin comes from the gradual increase in users, while traditional electronic money relies on legal currencies, which makes bitcoin's enjoy more room for value change. The value of Bitcoin is created depending on the number of people, goods and services which is willing to accept Bitcoin payments. If the number of people who accept Bitcoin increases, the market transactions of Bitcoin will further flourish, and Bitcoin will have huge room for appreciation. As there are only hundreds of thousands of people currently owning Bitcoin, compared with the one billion Internet users, there is a lot of room for growth, which is also an important reason for the strong confidence of most Bitcoin holders. However, if the number of Bitcoin users decreases, its value is also likely to fall.

4.8.2.The way how Bitcoin is made

The Bitcoin economy consists of a network of users' computers. The automatically adjusted algorithm releases 50 Bitcoins into the network every 10 minutes and gradually halves them until year 2140 whose automated growth rate is to ensure a regular increase in the money supply, which does not require the intervention of third parties, such as central banks that may cause hyperinflation.

4.8.3 The way how Bitcoin is mined

To prevent fraud, the Bitcoin software package has an anonymous public ledger that includes every transaction. Some Bitcoin users verify transactions by address cryptographic challenges, and the first solver will receive 50 new Bitcoins. Bitcoin can be stored in a virtual place, that is, a "wallet" in a desktop computer that is connected to the cloud for centralized services.

4.8.4 The way how Bitcoin is used

Once users download a Bitcoin program to their machine, using this currency is as easy as sending an email. The merchants who approve it are still few, but the number has been growing. They often look for traces of the Bitcoin logo on cash machines. Entrepreneurs who use Bitcoin are working to make Bitcoin transactions easier and do everything to choose from a designated service plan machine to a payment platform.

4.8.5 The way how Bitcoin is transacted

There are currently three levels of Bitcoin transactions.

The first is sending as a gift, in which novices can get a small amount of Bitcoin for free.

The second is a transaction in the foreign exchange market. Bitcoin can be exchanged with mainstream currencies at a floating ratio.

The third is consumption, which uses Bitcoin to complete purchases, and which includes many goods and services in the real economy.

4.8.6 Limitations of blockchain

Blockchain is an emerging technology that has many of the advantages we dream of. It will, however, also bring us some new troubles, which need us to grapple with in application. The following are some limitations of blockchain technology.

Without reference, large-scale data retrieval is difficult: Blockchain technology has a large amount of data, which grows exponentially. The scattered data will make related retrieval difficult.

Scope of smart contract program expression capabilities: The modeling of related data is still under discussion, especially how to describe and model some smart contracts.

Treatment of related problems after decentralization: Some related problems will emerge after decentralization. For example, the final confirmation mechanism requires a large amount of data calculation and decision-making mechanisms.

Long transaction confirmation time: When the blockchain is first installed, it will take a lot of time to download historical transaction data blocks. During transactions, in order to confirm the accuracy of the data, we will ask for some time to deal with the Internet. After getting confirmation from the entire network, the transaction is considered complete. Resource consumption issues: Resources including nodes, networks, and related platforms require a large amount of data to support them, so resource consumption is high, which increases costs.

High energy consumption problem: The overall energy consumption of the system is very large.

Pressure resistance when handling large-scale transactions: Large-scale transactions can cause network congestion. When it is severe, network collapse is incurred.

The problem of unchangeable mindset: Blockchain technology is built on the grassroots thinking of the Internet, which is very different from the traditional world's management values, and its initial development will be limited.

4.8.7 Innovation of the blockchain-led computing model

Before 2005, most systems were isolated and closed centralized network services. With the development of the Internet, the boundaries between them are gradually broken to form an open and centralized cloud service system. Each system works together to serve users. The trend of service in the future will be distributed, and decentralized. As a result, a more distributed, secure, and reliable service network comes into being, in which blockchain technology will play a very important role.

The integration of blockchain and cloud computing technology will eventually develop into an open and distributed cloud service architecture.

4.8.8 The future of blockchain

On the demand side, the fields such as finance, medical care, notarization, communication, supply chain, domain name, and voting have begun to realize the importance of blockchain and try to connect technology with the real world.

On the investment side, the supply of investment funds for the blockchain has gradually increased, and the enthusiasm for venture capital investment has continued to rise. The investment density is increasing. The supply of funds on the supply side is expected to promote the further development of technology.

On the market applications side, blockchain can become a market tool which can help society reduce platform costs and make intermediaries a thing of the past. Blockchain will promote the transfer of the company's existing business model focus and is expected to accelerate the company's development.

On the basic technology side, the blockchain is expected to promote the transformation of data recording, data dissemination, and data storage management methods; the blockchain itself is more like an open-source protocol at the bottom of the Internet, which will be touched or even replace the basic protocols of the existing Internet completely in the near future.

On the social structure side, blockchain technology is expected to integrate law and economy, completely subverting the original society's regulatory model; the organizational form will change due to it, and the blockchain may eventually lead people to distributed autonomous society.

The combination of blockchain and the internet of things unifies digital assets and original assets, narrowing the gap between consumer and cash assets, expanding the public's credit, and accelerating value circulation.

Blockchain may also develop as follows.

The intellectual property protection system is established on the blockchain, and the use of intellectual property is recorded across the entire network, and a global advertising market is established.

Blockchain + cloud computing can develop into a decentralized self-media and community system.

Blockchain can build a decentralized equity crowd funding system, allowing innovative projects to enter the circulation field in advance.

Blockchain can develop into a completely transparent financial management system.

Chapter 5 Artificial Intelligence

5.1 Definition

Artificial intelligence is an interdisciplinary discipline generated under the rapid development of science and technology and the emergence of new ideas, new theories, and new technologies. It involves mathematics, computer science, philosophy, cognitive psychology, information theory, and cybernetics and other disciplines. Generally speaking, artificial intelligence is a new technological science that researches and develops theories, methods, technologies, and application systems for simulating, extending, and expanding human intelligence, which is a branch of computer science that tries to understand the essence of intelligence and produce a new kind of intelligent machine that can respond in a similar way to human intelligence. Research in this area includes robotics, language recognition, image recognition, natural language processing and expert systems.

5.2 Technology layering

From the perspective of industrial practice, artificial intelligence can be divided into three layers: the basic layer, the technical layer and the application layer. The basic layer is closest to the "cloud" and the application layer the "end". The basic layer is the technology foundation for developing artificial intelligence relevant subdivision technologies such as big data, cloud computing, smart chips, sensors, and smart hardware. Big data provides the data foundation for the development of artificial intelligence. Artificial intelligence (AI), also known as intelligent machine or machine intelligence, refers to the intelligence expressed by machines made by humans. Usually artificial intelligence refers to the technology of presenting human intelligence through ordinary computer programs. The research on artificial intelligence is highly technical and professional, and its branches are in-depth and irrelevant. Therefore, it covers a wide range.

At the technical level, artificial intelligence technologies include image recognition, machine learning, knowledge atlas, speech recognition, biometric recognition, and natural language processing.

At the application level, artificial intelligence includes computational intelligence, perceptual intelligence, and cognitive intelligence. From the perspective of the development of the industrial chain, the basic layer of artificial intelligence is the foundation of building an industrial chain ecology, which has the highest hidden value, but requires long-term R&D and investment, and the financial burden for the enterprise cannot be underestimated. The application layer belongs to the solution layer which has the strongest monetization ability. The core technologies of artificial intelligence include machine learning, knowledge atlas, speech recognition, image recognition, biometric recognition, and natural language processing. Applications of artificial intelligence cover a wide range from computer science, financial trade, medicine, diagnostics, heavy industry, transportation, and telecommunications to online and telephone services, law, scientific discovery, toys and games, music and many more aspects.

Related sub-fields: machine learning, computer vision, real-time language translation, emotion-aware computing, gesture control, natural language processing, recommendation engine and collaborative filtering, intelligent robots, virtual personal assistants, and automatic recognition of video content.

5.3 Foundation

Perceived ability: Perceived ability is mainly realized through the internet of things. The internet of things refers to a huge network formed by combining various types of information sensing equipment in real time to collect any required information such as objects or processes that need to be monitored, connected, and interacted with the Internet. Its purpose is to realize the connection between things and things, things and people, all things and the network, and facilitate identification, management and control. A large number of sensors are installed on the internet of things to access the machine, which provides the interface and means for the machine equipment to sense and control the physical world. Through data collection, analysis, and transmission, it interacts and controls under manual intervention or automatic system operation. Perceived ability is the premise of the system's control and possession of information, and is the foundation of artificial intelligence work.

Comprehension: At this stage, the understanding of intelligent systems on things mainly depends on the processor's computational analysis capabilities, which is very different from humans' work through neuron analysis. Cloud computing integrates and optimizes various computing capabilities in the system through system settings, which greatly improves the computing and understanding capabilities of the system. Cloud computing mainly provides users with various services through the Internet. For different users, IaaS, PaaS, and SaaS'can be provided.

Artificial intelligence can be simply understood as a process of perception and decision-making. Its development requires three important foundations: data, computing power, and algorithms. Cloud computing is an important way to provide computing power, so cloud computing can be regarded as the foundation of artificial intelligence development.

Learning ability: Learning ability is an important driving force for the continuous improvement of artificial intelligence. The reason why artificial intelligence can solve problems autonomously under a variety of complex conditions, and the ability to solve problems continues to increase, is mainly artificial intelligence has strong self-learning capabilities, that is, machine learning capabilities. The method of machine learning is to use big data to abstract human experience in processing and solving problems, so big data is a book for artificial intelligence to carry out self-learning. There are different classification methods for machine learning based on different learning models, learning methods, and algorithms.

(1) Machine learning is classified into supervised learning, unsupervised learning, and reinforcement learning based on learning models.

Supervised learning is to use certain learning strategy/method to establish a model method to achieve labeling (classification) / mapping of new data / instances based on labeled limited training sets. The most typical supervised learning algorithms include regression and classification. Supervised learning requires that the classification labels of the training samples are known. The higher the accuracy of the classification labels, the more representative the samples, and the higher the accuracy of the learning model. Supervised learning has been widely used in the fields of natural language processing, information retrieval, text mining, handwriting recognition, and spam detection.

Unsupervised learning uses unlabeled limited data to describe the structure / law hidden in unlabeled data. The most typical unsupervised learning algorithms include single-class density estimation, single-class data dimensionality reduction, and clustering. Unsupervised learning does not require training samples and manually labeled data, which is convenient for compressing data storage, reducing the amount of calculations, improving the speed of the algorithm, and avoiding classification errors caused by positive and negative sample offsets. It is mainly used in economic forecasting, anomaly detection, data mining, image processing, pattern recognition and other fields, such as organizing large computer clusters, social network analysis, market segmentation, and astronomical data analysis.

Reinforcement learning is the learning of intelligent systems from environment to behavior reflection to maximize the value of the reinforcement signal function. Because the external environment provides little information, reinforcement learning systems must learn on their own experience. The goal of reinforcement learning is to learn the reflection from the state of the environment to the behavior, so that the body's choice of behavior can get the maximum reward from the environment, making the external environment evaluate the learning system in a certain sense as the best. It has been successfully applied in the fields of robot control, autonomous driving, chess, and industrial control.

(2) According to the learning method, machine learning can be divided into traditional machine learning and deep learning.

Traditional machine learning starts from some observation (training) samples and tries to discover the laws that cannot be obtained through principle analysis, so as to achieve accurate prediction of future data behaviors or trends. Related algorithms include logistic regression, hidden Markov method, support vector machine method, K nearest neighbor method, three-layer artificial neural network method, Adaboost algorithm, Bayesian method, and decision tree method. Traditional machine learning balances the effectiveness of learning results and the interpretability of learning models, and provides a framework for solving learning problems with limited samples. It is mainly used for pattern classification, regression analysis, and probability density estimation with limited samples. One of the important theoretical foundations common to traditional machine learning methods is statistics, which has been widely used in many computer fields such as natural language processing, speech recognition, image recognition, information retrieval, and biological information.

Deep learning is a learning method for building deep structure models. Typical deep learning algorithms include deep belief networks, convolutional neural networks, restricted Boltzmann machines, and recurrent neural networks. Deep learning is also called deep neural network (refers to neural networks with more than 3 layers). Deep learning, as an emerging field in machine learning research, was proposed by Hinton and his groups in 2006. Deep learning originates from multi-layer neural networks, and its essence is to give a way to integrate feature representation and learning into one. Deep learning is characterized by abandoning interpretability and simply pursuing the effectiveness of learning. After years of exploration and research, many models of deep neural networks have been produced, of which convolutional neural networks and recurrent neural networks are two typical models. Convolutional neural networks are often applied to spatially distributed data; recurrent neural networks introduce memory and feedback into neural networks and are often applied to temporally distributed data. The deep learning framework is the basic underlying framework for deep learning. It generally includes mainstream neural network algorithm models, provides stable deep learning APIs, and supports distributed learning of training models between servers, GPUs, and TPUs. Some frameworks also equip with the ability to run on multiple platforms, including mobile devices and cloud platforms, bringing unprecedented speed and practicality to deep learning algorithms. Currently the mainstream open source algorithm frameworks include TensorFlow, Caffe / Caffe 2, CNTK, MXNet, Paddle-paddle, Torch / PyTorch and Theano.

(3) In addition, common algorithms for machine learning include transfer learning, active learning, and evolutionary learning.

Machine learning refers to the use of algorithms already set to analyze and learn data, and use the data as a basis to judge future development trends and predict the possible future development results based on this. Machine learning algorithms include at least decision trees, logical induction programming, clustering algorithms, and Bayesian networks. Take the decision tree model for example. A computer uses historical data to make detailed dichotomy judgments, thereby forming a historical analysis based on predictive analysis of similar events that may occur in the future. With historical data, machine learning can be trained to obtain a running model based on historical data. Based on the model, it can predict the future according to the input data. The level of learning ability determines the scientific nature of the modeling and the accuracy of future predictions. Machine learning is a continuous process. Only by continuously entering data, the system automatically optimizes and adjusts the model to gradually improve the accuracy of the prediction. This is the meaning of learning ability.

Interaction ability: Human-computer interaction is the key to the success of artificial intelligence. In recent years, with the development of speech recognition technology, human interaction with computers through speech has gradually become a reality. The degree of development of interactive capabilities will ultimately determine whether artificial intelligence will promote human leapfrog development. Machine deep learning is the most important core technology of human-machine interaction. It is based on multi-layer neural networks, integrates machine self-learning, abstracts related concepts from a large number of samples, and makes judgments and decisions based on its own understanding. The most famous case of human-computer interaction is in the field of Go, the alpha dog developed by Google using artificial intelligence technology.

Human-computer interaction mainly studies the information exchange between humans and computers, mainly including the two parts of information exchange between humans and computers, which is an important peripheral technology in the field of artificial intelligence. Human-computer interaction is a comprehensive subject closely related to cognitive psychology, ergonomics, multimedia technology, and virtual reality technology. The traditional information exchange between humans and computers mainly depends on interactive devices, including keyboard, mouse, joystick, data clothing, eye movement tracker, position tracker, data gloves, pressure pen and other input devices, as well as output devices such as printers, graphics machine, display devices, helmet-mounted displays and speakers. Human-computer interaction technology, in addition to traditional basic interaction and graphic interaction, also includes voice interaction, emotional interaction, somatosensory interaction, and brain-computer interaction. The four types of typical interaction methods closely related to artificial intelligence are introduced below.

1.Voice interaction

Voice interaction is an efficient way of interacting. It is a comprehensive technology for humans to interact with computers using natural speech or machine-synthesized speech, combining knowledge in the fields of linguistics, psychology, engineering, and computer technology. Voice interaction should not only study voice recognition and synthesis, but also study the interaction mechanism and behavior of people in the voice channel. The voice interaction process includes four parts: speech collection, speech recognition, semantic understanding, and speech synthesis. Speech collection completes audio input, sampling, and encoding; speech recognition completes the conversion of speech information into machine-recognizable text information; semantic understanding completes the corresponding operation based on the characters or commands after speech recognition converted text; speech synthesis completes text information conversion to sound information. As the most natural and convenient way for humans to communicate and obtain information, voice interaction has more advantages than other interaction methods, which can bring fundamental changes to human-computer interaction. It is the commanding heights of the future development of the era of big data and cognitive computing, with vast development and application prospects.

2.Emotional interaction

Emotion is a high-level information transmission, while emotional interaction is an interactive state. It conveys emotions when expressing functions and information, evoking people's memories or inner feelings. Traditional human-computer interaction cannot understand and adapt to human emotions or moods without the ability to understand and express emotions. It is difficult for computers to have the same intelligence as humans, and to achieve true harmony and nature through human-computer interaction. Emotional interaction is to give computers the ability to observe, understand, and generate various emotions similar to humans, and ultimately to enable computers to interact naturally, graciously, and vividly like humans. Emotional interaction has become a hot topic in the field of artificial intelligence, which aims to make human-computer interaction more natural. At present, there are still many technical challenges in the processing of emotional interaction information, the description of emotions, the process of acquiring and processing emotional data, and the manner of expressing emotions.

3.Somatosensory interaction

Somatosensory interaction refers to the fact that the individual does not need any complicated control system, and directly interacts naturally with the surrounding digital equipment and environment through physical movements based on somatosensory technology. According to the different somatosensory methods and principles, somatosensory technology is mainly divided into three categories: inertial sensing, optical sensing and optical combined sensing. Somatosensory interaction is usually supported by a series of technologies such as motion tracking, gesture recognition, motion capture, and facial expression recognition. Compared with other interaction methods, somatosensory interaction technology has been greatly improved both in terms of hardware and software. The interactive devices develop towards miniaturization, portability, and convenience of use, which has greatly reduced the constraints on users and made interaction process more natural. At present, somatosensory interaction has been widely used in games and entertainment, medical assistance and rehabilitation, fully automatic 3D modeling, assisted shopping, eye movement tracker and other fields.

4.Brain-computer interaction

Brain-computer interaction is also called brain-computer interface, which means that it does not depend on neural channels such as peripheral nerves and muscles, and directly implements the pathway of information transmission between the brain and the outside world. The brain-computer interface system detects the activity of the central nervous system and converts it into manual output instructions, which can replace, repair, enhance, supplement or improve the normal output of the central nervous system, thereby changing the interaction between the central nervous system and the internal and external environment. Brain-computer interaction realizes the conversion of brain signals to machine instructions by decoding neural signals. Generally, it includes three modules: signal acquisition, feature extraction, and command output. From the perspective of EEP signal acquisition, brain-computer interfaces are generally divided into two categories: invasive and non-invasive. In addition, there are other common classification methods for brain-computer interfaces: according to the direction of signal transmission, they can be divided into brain-to-computer, computer-to-brain, and two-way brain-computer interfaces; according to the type of signal generation, they can be divided into spontaneous brain-computer interfaces and evoked brain-computer interface; according to different signal sources, they can be divided into brain-computer interface based on EEG, brain-computer interface based on functional MRI, and brain-computer interface based on near-infrared spectrum analysis.

5.4 Classification

According to the application of artificial intelligence, artificial intelligence can be divided into proprietary artificial intelligence, general artificial intelligence, and super artificial intelligence.

According to the connotation of artificial intelligence, artificial intelligence can be divided into human-like behavior (simulating behavior results), human-like thinking (simulating brain operation), and pan-intelligence (no longer limited to simulating humans).

At this stage, artificial intelligence is transitioning from proprietary artificial intelligence to general artificial intelligence. It is driven by the Internet technology cluster (data / algorithm / computing) and application scenarios to develop collaboratively and evolve itself. Artificial intelligence is no longer limited to simulating human behavior results. Instead, it has been extended to "pan-intelligent applications", that is, better problem solving, creatively solving problems and tackling more complex problems. These problems include not only the difficulties of information acceptance and processing faced by people in the era of information explosion, but also the problems of increasing operating costs faced by enterprises, changes in consumer demands and behavior models, and disruption of business models as well as challenges to the governance of nature and the environment, optimization of social resources, and maintenance of social stability.

5.4.1 Intelligent investment advisory practice

Robotic investment advisory, also known as automated digital wealth management solution and intelligent investment or intelligent financial management, is to provide investors with investment decision-making and investment consulting services through automated equipment and procedures, which can be automated or semi-automated to interact with wealth management clients to provide wealth management advice to customers online or online and offline. At the same time, they can automatically manage the funds invested by customers. In view of the fact that robotic advisors essentially provide investment decisions based on data, the book refers to robotic advisors as digital wealth management. According to its different meanings, digital wealth management is divided into narrow type and broad one. Narrow digital wealth management is to recommend stock investment portfolio and provide automated, intelligent, and personalized asset allocation advice services, and track and automatically adjust portfolios, based entirely on the preservation and appreciation of wealth and the investor's risk appetite, financial status, financial planning, and intelligent computer system calculation, and automation and intelligence; digital wealth management in a broad sense is a system considers the financial situation of investors and carries out precise allocation of their personal wealth, considers a variety of assets, such as stocks, funds, and insurance, and conducts scientific planning of investors' asset allocation. In addition to preserving and appreciating wealth, we will also plan and optimize investor personality and investment portfolios.

5.4.2 What is Robot-Adviser

Robot-Adviser, also known as robotic advisor, is an online investment advisory service model that combines modern portfolio theory (MPT) with emerging technologies such as big data, artificial intelligence, and cloud computing. Robot-Adviser builds quantitative trading decision models based on algorithms, valuations and trading models in the traditional financial sector, reducing manual intervention. Robot-Adviser uses online questionnaires and methods, combines investors' investment objectives, risk appetite, risk tolerance, financial status and other variables to automatically generate personalized and intelligent asset allocation solutions for customers through algorithms. Robot-Adviser provides customers with a combination of resource allocation such as stock allocation, stock option operation, bond allocation, real estate asset allocation, and provides services such as asset rebalancing, mortgage repayment, and transaction execution. It is aimed at providing customers with long-term stable income under controllable risks.

Robot-Adviser can optimize the penetration of investment advisers in the following three points

The first is to lower the investment service threshold and lower the investment threshold. The second is the method of Robot-Adviser based on online questionnaires and big data modeling to make customer portraits through multiple dimensions such as user income, gender, age, and psychological characteristics; the third is that Robot-Adviser uses algorithms to identify users' risk preferences and provides customers with differentiated investment solutions, which effectively solves the problem of high communication costs in the traditional investment advisory field and reduces communication costs, which in turn increases investor real returns.

5.4.3 Core features of Robot-Adviser

5.4.3.1 A digital business model centered on automation and technology

Smart Investment Advisor provides investors with financial investment advice through advanced electronic technology. In the development history of Robot-Adviser, it started with online marketing via mobile Internet, surveyed customers' investment needs through electronic questionnaires, and provided investment advice based on customers' investment needs. With the continuous development of big data and artificial intelligence, Robot-Adviser can provide customers with investment portfolios.

Services such as automatic rebalancing strategies and automatic generation of investment reports can also provide customers with additional services such as online financial management training and financial information exchange. In FOF's asset allocation process, rebalancing is one of the very important dynamic management links. After drawing strategic asset allocation (SAA) and tactical asset allocation (TAA), the operation of the combination will make the asset allocation ratio in it continuously change. Rebalancing is an important part of continuously revising to maintain asset allocation goals. Practice shows that rebalancing has obvious effects on reducing portfolio volatility and increasing portfolio Sharpe ratio.

Therefore, Robot-Adviser provides customers with a full range of digital and systematic services, making 24/7 service possible. Customers can experience the diverse functions of Robot-Adviser through any mobile Internet terminal, and track their asset accounts more effectively.

Robot-Adviser benefits from the automated daily life. They eliminate human intervention by automating the investment process, which reduces labor costs and lowers the service threshold. According to statistics from CapGemini Consulting, globally, 82.5% of high-net-worth individuals under the age of 40 want to manage their wealth through digital channels; among high-net-worth individuals over the age of 40, this proportion reaches 54.01%. 65% of wealthy people said that when choosing an asset management company, digital diversification and convenient asset management services are an important consideration after the return on investment. According to data from the National Financial Services Digital Survey, 42% of respondents said that convenience is one of the important reasons for choosing digital financial services. Compared with traditional investment advisory companies, digital financial services have become one of the advantages of intelligent investment advisory companies. With the advancement of digital processes, the intelligent investment consulting industry will be more favored by investors.

5.4.3.2 Distributed settings ETF

The so-called passive investment refers to an investment strategy based on a certain market index (such as the Shanghai Stock Exchange

Index, the US Dollar Index, the Dow Jones Index, and the Heng Seng Index) which is held for a long time. Passive investment management is a form of investment that seeks returns in broader market indices, sectors and regions. When a passive investment model tracks a benchmark index (the most basic and popular index that reflects the trading conditions of a stock exchange), or a well-formed subset, an active investment strategy attempts to follow certain rules, emotions, or the investment managers point of view to obtain returns higher than market by buying and selling certain stocks, that is, passive investment seeks to obtain beta returns (the portion of financial asset returns that fluctuates with the market is relative returns), while active investment pursues to win alpha returns (the part that does not fluctuate with the market is the absolute return).

Robot-Adviser provides customers with digital asset allocation services through big data and machine learning. Robot-Adviser uses passive investment strategies for value investment, and uses different types of ETFs as the main investment targets. It also increases the diversification of portfolios by implementing dynamic allocation of various types of ETFs, which effectively reduces the non-systematic risk of portfolios.

ETF (Exchanged Traded Funds), also known as trading open index funds or exchanges

A trading fund is an open-end fund that trades within the field and has variable fund shares. An index fund is to see a specific index as the target index (such as the S&P500 index), and the constituent stocks of the index are used as investment objects. The investment product is constructed by purchasing all or part of the constituent stocks of the index to track the performance of the targeting index.

Robot-Adviser uses ETFs to build long-term tax evasion investment portfolios to achieve the following goals: Minimize the price code of charges which severely hit the traditional financial advisory market; Automatically manage and rebalance the commercialization of investment portfolios; Simplify the performance reporting mechanism; By investing in more efficient financial products, reduce the cost of compliance inspection, risk control and data purchase; shift investors' eyes to market trends rather than individuals, making the investment decision-making process more bearable, more transparent, and more rational.

Robot-Adviser diversify non-systematic risks of customers by constructing investment portfolios, aiming at obtaining a stable portion of the beta of the market. Unlike active investment strategies, the investment objective of Robot-Adviser is not to obtain excess market returns. At the same time, the passive investment strategy followed by Robot-Adviser will not generate positive feedback to the market, which will help reduce market speculation, increase market effectiveness, and stabilize the financial market.

From the perspective of mature capital markets in the United States, as market efficiency continues to improve, it has become increasingly difficult to obtain the return that exceeds market performance. The fund industry has experienced closed-end funds, active-based funds, and multiple innovative funds (index-type funds, currency funds, tax-exempt funds, and alternative strategic funds). Since 2000, the fund industry has once again faced a major transformation, and passive products such as ETFs and FOFs have risen rapidly. As a digital asset allocation service, Robot-Adviser is driven by artificial intelligence technology represented by big data and machine learning algorithms, with different types of ETFs as the main investment targets, focusing on the allocation of large categories of assets to build "smart beta". This "active investment behavior" based on "passive products" has the notable characteristics of low fees, low thresholds, high efficiency, and high dispersion, which complies with the magnificent development trend of the big asset management industry.

Both financial literature and academic research have publicly criticized active funds by comparing active funds with passive funds. Robert Arnold, Andrew Belkin, and Ye Jia pointed out in a paper Invest Management Reflections in 2000 that within a 20-year time span, the pre-tax income of active funds averages are 2.1% lower than the vanguard standard Poole 500 Index annually. The failure of active funds is caused by a number of factors. First, active funds charge exorbitant fees to taxable investors, thus accounting for a portion of investors' net income. Second, active funds cannot restrain small-cap stocks and their security is impaired. Third, active transaction may bring more capital gains, but at the same time it will bring more tax payments which affects investors' after-tax returns. Therefore, the Robot-Adviser platform adopts a passive investment strategy by holding a basket of ETF funds with weak asset correlation, as well as reducing asset management costs and service commissions to gain investors' favor and outperform the market.

Take Vanguard, the largest intelligent investment company in the United States for example. Its investment logic has the following points: Because short-term market fluctuations cannot be predicted, but the market will develop upward in the long term, investment should be based on long-term value investment; Passive (index) investment is better than active investment, because only a few fund managers can outperform the index, fund managers are not as reliable as robots or indexes; Machine operations can effectively avoid irrational measures that fund managers may take when facing market fluctuations, and make up for short-term loss by long-term holdings; The investment consultant should consider all the client's assets in conjunction with the client's long-term financial goals (such as retirement plans) and provide targeted asset allocation services.

5.4.3.3 Investment portfolio auto-rebalancing strategy

Robot-Adviser is based on the customer's own financial management needs, using algorithms and products to complete the financial advisory services previously provided by humans. According to the set investment allocation ratio requirements, the Robot-Adviser will automatically adjust positions by buying and selling corresponding assets when the asset price in the investment portfolio changes with the market and the asset portfolio deviates from the allocation ratio, making investment settings reach target level again. Robot-Adviser can ensure that the investment portfolio follows its long-term investment goals through automated position adjustment strategies and avoid irrational operations by investors. In essence, portfolio rebalancing is a risk management technique, which refers to the strategy of adjusting the weight of various assets in time to achieve the initial target level of asset allocation of the portfolio when the current asset allocation of the portfolio deviates from the target allocation, making asset allocation return to long-term equilibrium, and the market often derails investment portfolios. Rebalancing is one of the important tools for portfolio management and risk control, helping to ensure that investment plans are aligned with their investment objectives. Robot-Adviser tries to help users overcome the market cycle through its most typical investment strategies characterized by long-term and automatic rebalancing, because they believe in the assumption that long-term investment returns depend on the proportion of asset allocation.

5.4.3.4 Personalized decisions, goals and behaviors

The goal of Robot-Adviser is not to bring excess returns to users, but to use a series of intelligent algorithms and portfolio optimization theoretical models based on differentiated asset allocations such as risk tolerance levels, return targets, and style preferences provided by individual investors to match the investment portfolio with the user's risk tolerance and risk appetite, thereby avoiding misoperations caused by the emotions of investment managers or customers, and stabilizing investment returns. The personalized investment experience that crosses individual goals and personality given by intelligent investment consulting is the most eye-catching and most challenging feature. It is this feature that attracts radical technology innovation companies and mature companies in the industry to spend big in its research and development. Creating a truly disruptive and emotional dialogue between investors and technology companies is the tipping point for the intelligentization of the financial industry.

Traditional wealth management managers mainly use paper questionnaires to record the investment trajectory of each investor, while Robot-Adviser uses electronic technology to reshape the registration process and improve the user experience. The vast majority of market allocations are based on the assumption that investors are rational and risk-averse, and only higher expected incomes allow them to take on higher risks. Therefore, the essential difference between traditional wealth management managers and Robot-Adviser is not that they have different understandings of risk assumptions, but that Robot-Adviser makes the process of appraisal of risk appetite more attractive and enhance the sense of participation in the decision-making process of investors. The self-assessment results of the investor on the portfolio model are not so much the suggestions of the third party after considering the age, risk tolerance and expected return in a comprehensive way as the rational choices of investors themselves. For wealth management managers and Robot-Adviser, the most important thing to solve is that only continuous and transparent investor goals and fear-inducing mechanisms are the guarantee of the robustness and adaptability of the automated investment follow-up process. Only comprehensive and informative risk assessment process can successfully guide other areas of personal finance.

5.4.4 Robot-Adviser's theory foundation

5.5.4.1 Markowitz's Modern Portfolio Theory

Portfolio theory is divided into narrow sense and broad sense. Portfolio theory in the narrow sense refers to Markowitz's portfolio theory.

The financial theory of Robot-Adviser is based on MPT (Modern Portfolio Theory) proposed by Nobel Laureate in Economics in 1952 (Modern Portfolio Theory) Hary Markowitz.

The theory contains two important contents: the mean-variance analysis method and the portfolio effective boundary model.

Modern portfolio theory is the theoretical basis of all asset allocation models. Later, through extension of this theory by William. Sharpe and others, a complete theoretical system was formed. Today, portfolio theory based on modern portfolio theory is commonly used by various financial professional institutions, private banks, sovereign wealth funds and pension funds.

1.Returns and risks of a single security

Measuring the risk of a single security can be expressed in the degree of dispersion of expected returns in the future return level. The weighted average of the various possible returns of the security and the corresponding probability is the expected value, and the risk is calculated by the variance or standard deviation.

2.Investment portfolio

Two relevant characteristics of a portfolio are:

Its expected rate of return

The possible rate of return revolves around a measure of its expected deviation, where variance is the easiest to analyze as a measure.

3.Returns and risks of the investment portfolio

Its due to the dual needs of security and profitability, and the combination of risk assets and risk-free assets. To meet the security need, risk-free assets need to be combined. For profitability, risky assets need to be combined. The second level of combination considers how to combine risk assets. Since any two assets with poor correlation or negative correlation will have a risk return greater than the risk return of the individual asset, it is possible to continuously combine assets with poor correlation and keep the effective front of the portfolio away from risk.

4.No difference curve

According to the preference rules, some securities portfolios cannot be distinguished from good or bad. In this way, a given investor, given any securities portfolio, can get a series of securities portfolios with the same degree of satisfaction (no difference) according to their preferences, forming an indifference curve. The investor's attitude towards the expected return and risk will change, and different comparison results will be obtained. Selecting this investor will have a cluster of indifference curves.

5.Application of MPT theory in the field of Robot-Adviser

Robot-Adviser adopts the strategy of asset allocation plus passive management. Asset allocation uses the technology of machine learning modeling and uses supervised and unsupervised learning methods to perform dynamic and multi-dimensional analysis of asset market products in real time and accurately. Then based on modern portfolio theory, the correlation between different assets and asset risk factors, an optimal and effective front-end investment portfolio is built, to achieve high-precision judgment of the market to enhance returns, and build fully automated investment management process featuring data collection, processing, learning, training, and return for measurement and improvement, configuration and adjustment.

There are many types of securities in the market, and different products have different risks and expected returns characteristics. The purpose of asset allocation is to disperse assets into diversified securities products. The variance of the expected return on a security is used here to describe the security risk.

Future returns are uncertain and a random variable, so a certain value cannot be used to describe the rate of return. Random variables are generally described by probability distributions. Two important numerical characteristics of a probability distribution are mean and variance.

Mean variance analysis uses the mean of a probability distribution when describing the rate of return. Since the mean is also called a mathematical expectation, this description is called the expected return, which is written as E (R). In describing the risk, the variance of the probability distribution is used, which is written as Var (E). Variance represents the degree of dispersion in the distribution, which is just a description of uncertainty. According to the knowledge of probability distribution:

All investment portfolios composed of risk and return are one point. Among them, the outermost points form a curve, which is called the effective frontier curve. (For a given rate of return (mean), the portfolio on this curve has the smallest risk (variance). This curve is the effective boundary, also known as the effective frontier.)

The optimal asset allocation point falls on the effective frontier curve. From a vertical perspective, it is the investment portfolio that investors can obtain maximum profits under the conditions of risk determination. From a horizontal perspective, it is the minimum investment risk portfolio that investors can obtain when the expected level of return is determined.

As the premise of the theory is that the combination of small variance with the same return rate (small risk with the same return) and high return with the same variance (high profit with the same risk), there is a minimum variance combination at each risk point. The solid line that connects these points is the Efficient Frontier. Combined with the efficient frontier, and according to the degree of investor's risk appetite, an optimal investment portfolio based on the degree of investor's risk appetite can be constructed.

The investment objective of Robot-Adviser is to help investors configure their investment portfolios by diversifying their investments, so that investors can obtain the maximum portfolio returns under controllable risks.

Investing in a single asset will cause huge risks. Therefore, as the saying goes, you can't put all your eggs in one basket. For example, if an investor invests all of his funds in a single stock, the risk that investors need to take when the stock soars and plummets is very large. If investors invest all the funds in proportion to different stock funds, bonds, and currency funds, the yield of their entire investment portfolio will be greatly reduced by the impact of single market fluctuations. Therefore, a reasonable portfolio of asset allocation, and scientific funds investment into different securities can meet the requirements of investors' risk tolerance and return expectations. Risks wane, and returns wax in different types of securities. Long-term investment portfolios can provide investors with long-term investment returns.

The Robot-Adviser process includes the five steps of user portrait, asset allocation, portfolio construction, transaction execution, and rebalancing. The various types of investment-only advisory products in the market basically follow the process as shown below:

Compared with traditional personal investment, Robot-Adviser pay more attention to income (the investors bear the profits brought by market risks), so asset allocation and investment portfolio construction play an important role in the entire Robot-Adviser service. Obtaining stable and efficient beta returns through the "smart" method is the core competitiveness of Robot-Adviser products.

Based on its large asset portfolio capacity and low time sensitivity, Robot-Adviser can meet the requirements of small investors to diversify capital risks, which can enable small-amount investors to diversify their risks through asset allocation to obtain market beta returns.

5.4.4.2 Black-Litterman model

The Black-Litterman type is also called the mean variance model, or tilt optimization model, which was first proposed by Fisher Black and Robert Litterman in 1902 and is based on the financial industry optimization of research and application of the Markowitz model over the decades. The Black-Litterman model further develops on the basis of Markowitz's optimization theory of mean variance. It uses probabilistic statistical methods to combine investors' views on large assets with market equilibrium returns to generate new expected returns, and market returns and individual investors' views were included in the scope of the model review, and the expected returns were calculated again. This model can be based on market benchmarks, and investors can make propensity opinions on certain large-scale assets. Then, the model will propose suggestions for the allocation of the major assets based on the propensity opinions of investors. The new asset allocation has an intuitive combination and understandable weight allocation. The Black-Litterman model adds the calculated expected return rate into the mean variance model to obtain the optimized asset allocation. The Black-Litterman model combines prior information with historical information. It is a typical Bayesian analysis method that has gradually been accepted by the mainstream on the Wall Street. It has now become the main asset allocation tool of the asset management department of Goldman Sachs.

The Third Part

Application of the Financial Industry

Chapter 6 Application of Banking

6.1 Data

6.1.1 Banks actively participate to expand data sources

(1) The financial industry is a data-intensive industry. Whether it is a traditional offline business or a new type of online business, a key element of its competition is still data. Faced with new business operation models, personal payment habits, and the infiltration of emerging financial forces, traditional financial institutions represented by banks have begun to take proactive measures to respond.

(2) The banking industry has made a foray into e-commerce, collect data directly, create various platforms belonging to banks, obtain customers, information and business through the platform, hold the platform data in its own hands, and grasp the leading power of the industrial chain.

(3) At present, the Chinese banking industry already has a large number of valuable data resources, such as real-name identity information and personal and corporate credit data, but it is not comprehensive enough, and other customer information such as personality characteristics, hobbies, lifestyles, industry fields and family status is not in the hands of the bank. In addition, a variety of heterogeneous data is difficult to analyze and process, such as information on bank customer funds exchange, behavior information on customer web browsing, voice information for service calls, and video recording information of Service

Hall and ATMs. In the era of big data, banks need to improve their own data mining and analysis capabilities. To this end, banks began to expand the scope of data collection and develop data resources. There are three types of models for banks in expanding data collection:

①Large banks (ICBC, CCB, Bank of Communications, etc.) begin to build their own e-commerce platforms

a. In terms of e-commerce services, Shanrong Commerce provides B2B and B2C customer operation models, covering the fields of commodity wholesale, commodity retail, and house transactions.

b. In terms of financial services, the platform provides customers with a full range of financial services from payment settlement, deposit, guarantee to financing services.

c. The main purpose of CCB is to break the transaction payment settlement information monopolized by online e-commerce and third-party payment through building the platform. It not only becomes the end of the payment chain, but also captures the customer's transaction data from the source, making the data important basis for the bank in the future to rate customer credit.

②Build various network platforms to enhance traditional banking business

a. Establish a supply chain financial platform: Through the collection and integration of business flows, logistics, capital flows, and information flows generated from the business activities of relevant parties, it provides comprehensive financing and value-added services such as online financing, settlement, investment and wealth management that is suitable for the entire supply chain.

b. Establish an online exchange platform for financial institutions to promote information exchange between institutions and the marketing of financial products: Industrial Bank's "Bank-to-Bank Platform" has comprehensively improved its counterpart business by creating online and offline platforms. It integrates the Industrial Bank's own resources to establish a professional, complete and flexible product and service system. It started from an Internet connection and agent access to a modern payment system business. It has developed into complete financial service solutions to the eight businesses of technology management output services, capital and asset-liability structure optimization services, and foreign exchange agency services.

③Promote system and model innovations such as cross-border integration, scenario embedding, and O2O finance to explore new engines for business transformation and development.

a. A typical example is direct selling banks. Under this business model, banks have no business outlets and do not issue physical bank cards. Customers obtain banking products and services mainly through remote channels such as computers, email, mobile phones, and telephones.

b. Since there are no branch operating expenses and management costs, direct selling banks can provide customers with more competitive deposit and loan prices and lower commission rates, so they can provide customers with more convenient and preferential financial services than traditional banks.

6.1.2 About data developing

The bank also cooperates with various data analysis professional firms to comprehensively process and analyze the existing "big data" of the bank.

6.1.2.1 Application of big data in bank risk management

(1) With the development of information technology, the risks

faced by banks are becoming more and more complicated and changeable. Mastering more data and performing reasonable processing have become the key to effectively manage risks of banks. The specific risks are:

①Sources of external risks are increasingly diversified: In addition to traditional banking customers such as industrial and commercial enterprises, residents, and counterpart banks, emerging market leaders such as small loan companies, guarantee agencies, shadow banks, and private financing will all become sources of risk. External risk events are volatile, complex, and difficult to identify, which are likely to pass risks to the bank, which will have an adverse effect on the sound bank.

②The spread speed of risks is accelerated, and external risk events may promptly trigger systemic risks: With the use of technologies such as the Internet, big data, and cloud computing, the links of all market leaders such as banks, enterprises, intermediaries, and technology service providers are getting closer and closer, the transmission channels of risks are diversifying, the speed of transmission is accelerating, and part risks are likely to spread rapidly within the system. Individual events may be quickly passed through We Chat, Weibo and other channels, or even exaggerated, causing banks to face greater credit risk.

③Banks face technical risks: In recent years, cyber security incidents have occurred frequently, and computer viruses can spread quickly through the Internet. Once a program is infected by a virus, the entire computer or even the integrated transaction Internet will receive the threat of the virus, which is extremely destructive. In traditional financial business, computer technology risk will only bring partial impact and loss. In Internet financial business, technical risks may cause systemic risks to the entire financial system, and then trigger the collapse of the system.

(2) With the explosive growth of data, centralized massive data storage can facilitate data analysis and processing, but improper security management can easily cause information leakage, loss, and damage. The increasingly developed Internet and information technology make the theft of information no longer require physical and compulsory intrusion into the system. Therefore, higher requirements for the security management capabilities of big data are proposed. With the introduction of cloud services, most organizations store some important data in the cloud of the Internet. Once the cloud data center has disaster, it will cause the loss of important customer data and bring all organizations' business to a halt. At present, China's ability to protect big data is very limited, the protection awareness and measures for data resources are relatively weak, and personal or corporate information being exposed to the Internet is a very common phenomenon. Its difficult to control the phenomenon of malicious acquisition and use of big data, which poses huge challenges to Internet finance security.

6.1.2.2 Big data and credit risk management

(1) Banks have developed a set of credit risk management methods in their long-term operations.

These methods run through every step of the bank's credit business. Starting with the screening of potential customers, banks use information collection and analysis to exclude high-risk customers. After determining the loan, the bank effectively prevented customers from engaging in high-risk investment activities through routine credit inspection and supervision and signing of loan contracts with restrictive terms with customers. In addition, banks require customers to provide collateral or guarantees for loans, keeping customers from defaults. In order to obtain as much information as possible, the bank and the customer have established long-term customer contacts, and any complaints in the operation of the customer will be passed on to the bank loan officer, reducing the cost of identifying customers and monitoring the cost of loans for banks. With the development of risk management technology, banks have developed credit risk measurement models, which require banks to obtain enough information and data, and effective process them, so that banks have a full understanding of their own risk status.

(2) The construction of a big data system can help banks better measure credit risk

a. Collecting data through multiple channels and methods can help banks obtain more comprehensive, three-dimensional, accurate, and timely information from borrowers, reducing the risk of information asymmetry. When engaged in credit business, banks must collect external data information through various methods and channels.

b. Using big data technology and related models can help banks discover new correlations between variables and provide a more accurate and fair basis for bank decisions.

c. With the continuous accumulation of multi-dimensional data, banks can build big data technology platforms and keep improving big data analysis technologies to help banks carry out risk model and provide them with a wider range of risk analysis and management tools.

6.1.2.3 Big data and operational risk management

(1) Risk factors banks need to pay special attention to include fraud, transaction process and transaction volume, interest rates, complexity of financial products and services, date effects, changes in operations, and complacency in management. Finally, they should determine how many important loss events are.

(2)The collection of data is an important part of operational risk management. Big data platform provides support for banks to build quantitative risk models.

a. Big data platform expands bank data sources. Banks can analyze risk events from multiple dimensions. A variety of non-traditional channels such as the Internet, mobile platforms and social media have become data sources.

b. Big data information is strongly effective for a given period of time and makes up for the shortcomings of traditional data sources. Banks can use the big data platform to collect data on operational risk events, understand changes in risk events in a timely manner, and improve the efficiency and effectiveness of operational risk management.

c. Make risk management more forward-looking. The big data platforms provide technical support for early detection of risk warning signals. Based on this, they take proactive risk management measures.

6.1.2.4 Big data achieves accurate risk control

(1)Big data can better address information asymmetry in traditional credit risk management, improve pre-loan risk measurement and post-loan risk early warning capabilities, and achieve precise and forward-looking risk management.

(2)In the era of big data, the banking industry can overcome the disadvantage of information. By binding user data, collecting user transaction information, removing data barriers, integrating users' online and offline data resources, and sharing various user information such as location information, it draws user pictures from multiple dimensions such as wealth, security, consumption and social interaction, establishes user credit reports, assesses credit risks, more fully reflects the financial status of individuals, families, and enterprises and predict risk events in a timely manner, reducing credit risks.

(3)Big data plays a huge role in identifying fraudulent transactions and anti-money laundering in banks. Banks can use the basic information, transaction history, historical behavior patterns and ongoing behavior patterns of customers to conduct real-time transaction anti-fraud analysis, in combination with intelligent rule engines .

6.1.3 Application of big data in bank customer expansion and maintenance

6.1.3.1 More customers to achieve precise marketing

(1)Banks need to analyze the data collected by their own businesses, and integrate external data to deepen their understanding of customers, mainly including customer behavior data on social media and social commentary. By combining the bank's internal data with external socialized data, the bank can obtain a more complete customer puzzle, thereby conducting more accurate marketing and management.

(2)If the bank has the data of the upstream and downstream of the industry chain where the company is located, it can better grasp the development of the company's external environment, so that it can predict the future situation of the company.

(3)Accurate bank marketing:

①Dynamic marketing which refers to marketing based on the customer's current status. For example, targeted marketing is conducted based on information such as the customer's location and recent consumption records; or events that change the state of life are considered marketing opportunities.

②Cross-marketing which refers to cross-selling different businesses or products to customers. For example, China Merchants Bank can effectively identify small and micro enterprise customers based on customer transaction record analysis, and then use remote banks to implement cross-selling.

③Personalized services which refers to the fact that banks can analyze customer preferences based on big data models and then make personalized recommendations to customers. For example, customers are accurately positioned according to the customer's age, shopping preferences and risk preferences to analyze their potential financial service needs, therefore conducting targeted marketing promotion.

④Customer life cycle management includes acquisition of new customers, prevention of customer loss, and success of winning back customers.

6.1.3.2 Data mining

1.Concept

It is a new business information processing technology. Its main characteristics are: extracting valuable information from a large amount of information data, transforming, analyzing, and modeling it to obtain useful data that is helpful to business decision-making.

The use of data mining technology by banks first needs to establish a unified central customer database to improve the ability to analyze customer information. The bank uses data mining technology in combination with various statistical analysis methods such as non-linear regression analysis, discriminant analysis and cluster analysis with the help of massive data, through data processing methods such as cleaning, conversion and loading to spot the associations and trends between the data, and tap other business laws and patterns that its difficult for methods to observe, so as to complete the tasks of data analysis, knowledge discovery, decision support and financial intelligence of big data, and predict the future behaviors of customers.

2.Data mining technology

(1)Data mining can help banks determine the personality characteristics of customers, thereby providing targeted services to customers

(2) Help banks to discover common characteristics of customers who purchase certain types of financial products, which can expand their business

(3)Discover the general characteristics of lost customers, and help banks to take targeted measures to avoid customer loss before customers with similar characteristics are lost.

According to the customer information and the relevant network footprint, the bank finds the customer's personality characteristics and other attributes and their related relationships through mining and analysis of big data, summarizes the customer's preferences, and conducts accurate and targeted marketing to improve marketing efficiency and quality.

3.Impact of big data analysis on banks

(1)According to big data analysis, banks can track problems existing in customer operations in real time and develop countermeasures in a timely manner

(2) Through data mining and analysis of customer operations, banks can discover causation in business data, make accurate judgments on customer operations, and formulate effective financial service strategies

Through big data analysis, banks can summarize the transaction habits and hobbies of different customers, and adopt cross-selling or value-added sales strategies to provide customers with personalized and differentiated services, which not only makes banks more recognized by customers, but also improves the bank's revenue.

Through data mining, banks can find problems existing in services in a timely manner and provide a basis for effectively improving service levels. For example, the bank obtains a large amount of data through the customer service system and conducts mining analysis to accurately take aim at the customer's consumption and investment needs and meet customer demands in a timely manner, thereby laying a foundation for improving customer satisfaction and service quality.

Through collecting and analyzing customers' financial data, credit records, and transaction records, banks identify customer quality, and measure customer spending power, repayment capability, and default probability to help banks build intelligent models that effectively distinguish customer quality, bringing convenience for improvement of bank asset quality and prevention of credit risks.

6.2 Mobile

With the development of mobile communication technology, the services provided by banking institutions have been extended, breaking the boundaries of time and space, improving the ability of bank financial services, and becoming a new profit model.

6.2.1 Impact of mobile communication technology development on banking model

1.The rapid development of mobile Internet has transformed the business model from the traditional counter model to e-commerce and mobile commerce. Correspondingly, the service model of commercial banks has also shifted from traditional bank outlets to self-service equipment and Network migration, mobile finance will become an important channel for banks to expand their business in the future.

Table 6-1

Commerce business	characteristics	Bank operation models
Traditional business	Merchants and customers communicate face-to-face, which has good interactivity; transactions need to be made in physical stores, and both parties need to conclude transactions at the same time and place. The corresponding costs are high, transactions are limited by time and place, and products are mainly physical	Banks mainly provide face-to-face services for customers with traditional physical branches and counter employees.
E-commerce	Transaction is made through the Internet, and transaction costs are low and the range of transactions is wide, including not only physical goods, but also virtual products	Banks focus on online banking and non-counter services
Circulation commerce	It is real-time, not limited by time and space, and can carry out business activities anytime and anywhere, but is limited by the coverage of the mobile network; transaction costs are low, efficiency is high with a wide range of transaction scope	Banks use mobile financial services as the main model

(2)4G advantages:

①The network speed is fast and the spectrum is wide. The network downloads files, pictures, and videos very fast, and has an excellent network experience.

②Integrate multiple services completely. A smart phone is more like a small computer, changing the user's perception of the mobile phone, forming the habits of mobile phone consumption, mobile entertainment, and social networking, and also allowing banking services to enter a new mobile era.

③The space provided for value-added services has grown. 4G is not just a technology, but also a combination of multiple technologies. With these technologies, people can realize wireless communication value-added services such as wireless local loop (WLL) and digital audio broadcasting (DAB).

④The above advantages of 4G networks help banks' financial services to become mobile. Services such as identity verification and face recognition can be implemented with the remote video function of 4G networks, which greatly improves the efficiency of bank service customers and the security of authentication, expanded the service scope of banks, extended finance to business and living areas, and formed a mobile financial ecological chain.

6.2.2 Direction of commercial banks' mobile development

1.Mobile payment and mobile banking

(1)Near field payment technology is the foundation of mobile payment, which is transformed from non-contact RFID and interconnection technologies. Combining the functions of inductive card reader, inductive card and point-to-point, it can exchange data with compatible devices over short distances. The proportion of NFC-enabled mobile phones is constantly increasing. In many cases, people can use NFC mobile phones to pay, such as subways, gas stations, and supermarkets.

(2)In addition to NFC payment, QR code payment has also been favored by users, which is a mobile payment solution based on an account system where merchants can compile transaction information such as accounts and product prices into a two-dimensional code and users can scan it with a mobile phone client side to pay to the merchants. Many domestic banks have added the "Scan QR Code" function to the mobile phone client source APP, which supports customers to pay in various cases such as mobile phone scan or being scanned, which can be used for mutual transfer payment between individual customers and can also enable small shops and vendors to generate QR codes to collect payments, and support bar code scanning gun.

①The Dragon Payment page of China Construction Bank has functions such as AA collection and scanning

②ICBC's QR code payment products can cover online and offline and all O2O payment cases

③Agricultural Bank of China launched K-code payment; Bank of Communications launched "Cloud Flash Payment" and "limafu";

④Postal Savings Bank of China, China Minsheng Bank and Ping An Bank also successively launched two-dimensional code transfer payment

(3) The faster transmission speed of the 4G network has greatly improved the user experience of mobile banking. The innovation of short-range transmission technology of terminals has made it possible for mobile phone users to make short-distance payments, which has made it more convenient for customers to pay. In this context, commercial banks have accelerated their mobile terminal layout. From We Chat Bank to mobile banking client side, all banks are actively exploring, vigorously promoting and marketing. At the same time, users' dependence on mobile and We Chat banking is also increasing and the bank's out-of-counter rate will continue to rise in the future. With the development of security technology and the popularity of mobile Internet and

smart phones, the number of mobile banking users will continue to grow rapidly.

2.Diversified mobile financial scenario layout

(1) With the rapid popularization and application of mobile Internet, the application scope of commercial banks' mobile finance is also expanding. Starting from payment and account management, financial management, insurance and credit are continuously integrated into people's basic necessities. The types of mobile financial products are getting richer. In the process of competing with Internet finance companies, banks are also actively learning from it, constantly improving their mobile application and embedding mobile finance in more scenarios.

(2) In the future, commercial banks will leverage their advantages in financial services and scenario construction through their own development or cross-border cooperation with other institutions to jointly provide customers with scenario-based financial services and build online financial services into a one-stop service platform support customers.

6.3 Intelligent

6.3.1 Concept

It refers to an app about the integration of modern communication with information technology, computer network technology, industry technology and intelligent control technology. The internet of things, big data, biometrics, artificial intelligence, and virtual reality technology have begun to be applied in banks, and the future of bank intelligence is infinite.

6.3.2 Application of intelligent technology

The internet of things is a physical network covering all things based on computer network construction centering the electronic code of the product, using radio frequency identification, invalid data communication and other technologies.

With the advancement of information technology, information sensors such as infrared sensors, global positioning systems, and laser scanners connect any item to the Internet, enabling intelligent identification, positioning, tracking, monitoring, and management.

Use of internet of things:

(1)The application of the internet of things in banks is mainly in the payment field, credit business and customer security. For example, during pre-loan surveys, banks can access the company's internal management system through the internet of things to accurately check corporate information to reduce the bank's credit risks. According to the identification equipment on the counter and self-service equipment, the safety of customer property can be ensured through biometric technology such as fingerprint and iris.

(2)Biometrics help banks better verify customer identity. The wide use of sensors and somatosensory technology has made commercial applications of human-computer interaction possible. Interactive devices such as intelligent robots can use gestures, voice, background graphics and sound processing technology to change the communication between machines and humans from a menu style to interactive communication, enhancing the applicability of self-service devices in interaction, improving the system's automatic service abilities, guiding customers to complete their business on their own, and catering to customers' online social behavior habits in the mobile Internet era.

(3) Big data technology helps banks achieve precise marketing,

conduct risk management, and discover new business opportunities. Big data helps banks better understand the personality characteristics of customers. According to the customer's gender, age, occupation, financial status, behavior habits and other data, it has a 360-degree panorama of the entire product, all channels, all relationship chains, and the entire life cycle for customers to carry out data insight and mining, and then form a customized product. When customers visit a network or website, personalized promotion was carried out to reduce customer decision-making costs, thereby increasing the success rate of sales and achieving precise marketing. In addition, big data enables banks to obtain customer information that could not be obtained under the traditional model. Through data mining and other technologies, banks can obtain information on changes in customer risk conditions in a timely manner, help banks make reasonable decisions in pre-loan assessments and give risk early warning signals in post-loan management process.

Augmented reality technology is a new technology that seamlessly integrates real-world with virtual-world information. It combines physical information (visual information, sound, taste, and touch) that are originally difficult to experience in a certain time and space in the real world through simulation and then overlay it, applies virtual information to the real world to be sensed by human, so as to achieve a sensory experience beyond reality. Virtual Reality (VR) technology is a computer simulation system that can create and experience a virtual world. It uses a computer to generate a simulation environment, which is system simulation of entity behaviors integrating various information as well as an interactive three-dimensional dynamic view. Augmented reality technology makes banks' smart branches interesting. For example, some banks use AR technology in the glass curtain wall of their smart branches, and customers can interact with the animated images on the screen. 3D virtual display technology is three-dimensional virtual reality technology. By naked eye 3D and other technologies, many financial products can be changed from two-dimensional flat images to three-dimensional scenes, helping customers to obtain more intuitive and interesting visual experience of products and making customers feel like being immersive.

6.3.3 Creating smart branches

(1)Compared with traditional branches, bank intelligent branches can better leverage the synergy of online and offline channels, combining virtual services with physical branches.

(2)Intelligent transformation of business, equipment and services has become an effective way for financial institutions to self-innovate and meet challenges.

(3)Intelligent pre-processing terminals, intelligent channel distribution systems, and intelligent interactive desktops are also put into use at bank branches. Face recognition and virtual reality technologies are used as new means to enrich marketing, improve customer service, and enhance user experience.

(4)Bank's measure to resolve the monotonous type of business:

①Use multimedia methods to improve the brand marketing of banks and customers' understanding of bank products and services.

②Strengthen the development of smart device functions.

③Optimize the layout of branches and business processes to achieve higher service efficiency and improve customer experience.

(5)Use of bank intelligent pre-processing terminal

①Customers can book offline services online saving times for calling, queuing, and filling orders.

②Through the intelligent channel shunting system, customers are effectively shunted to online channels and self-service machines to effectively reduce the load pressure on branches.

(6)The way that intelligent network breaks the barriers of traditional channels

Rebuild the bank's service processes and models through intelligent technology to provide customers with a better experience.

①When it comes to specific operations, you can add remote devices such as VITM, self-service card issuers, and self-service filling machines through intelligent network to create an intelligent service platform to realize the business model of "customer self-help" and "on-site review", and promote out-the-counter of transaction processing, streamlined business processes, integrated product marketing, expand self-service business scope, and improved service abilities.

②After the customer came to the bank's business branches, it guided the customer to smart devices for self-service transactions and self-selected products. The staff at the bank branches became "customer service specialists", who provided instructions on operations and introduced banking products according to customer characteristics.

③The intelligent service model will change the "counter employee operation" to "customer self-completion" and "customer around the counter" to "counter employee around the customer", ultimately making customer more satisfied.

(7)Development of Smart Branches

①It uses multimedia methods to enhance the brand marketing efforts of banks and customers' understanding of bank products and services. For example, Bank of China has set up a special customer experience area in its smart branches and placed different multimedia devices, allowing customers to scan through local news, market data, bank products and service information. In front of the large touch screen, customers can make actions such as zooming or panning by the arm to browse information or participate in financial games. The precious metal display stand uses holographic projection and 3D imaging technology. After the customer clicks the precious metal products label, the three-dimensional image will be displayed in front of peoples eyes in 360-degree rotation, with very realistic visual effects which can display detailed product information.

② Strengthen the development of smart device functions. The standard remote video or virtual teller machine at smart branches is a new type of complex service such as bank card application, activation, customer data maintenance, and written loss reporting, which enables remote tellers to conduct banking services for customers online using network video technology, which replaces complicated services that originally can only be face-to-face signing at branches counters. VTMs are still exploring globally, and Chinese banks are already leading in this regard.

③Optimize branches layout and business processes to achieve higher service efficiency and create a better customer experience. For example, business branches can be divided into multiple areas, each of which intelligent pre-processing terminals are allocated to use them to identify customers and perform business shunting, with the function of queuing. In terms of self-service order filling, customers can swipe their ID cards on the smart calling number pre-processing machine to transfer personal information to the counter employee's operating system, saving customers time to fill in the forms manually.

6.3.4 Building a smart bank

Smart banks are not just about the use of smart self-service equipment. Smart branches, in fact, are part of smart banks. In the future, smart banks will require banks to combine the establishment of hardware equipment and software systems with the optimization of internal bank processes. Optimizing the relationship between banks and customers based on the full channels and intelligence is a complex systematic project.

Smart banking is not a concept that has only recently emerged. It was mentioned in the article more than two decades ago, but the continuous advancement of technology has expanded the boundaries of smart banking.

What customers need is not the physical business base, but the functions of the bank. In the construction of smart banks, the application of intelligent technology has continuously reduced the service cost of the bank and also continuously improved the service efficiency.

The impact of new technologies on banks is divided into four stages

(1) Internet and social media customers handle business through online banking, and banks interact with customers through social media

(2)"Screens and mobile terminals" are ubiquitous, and customers handle transactions other than cash on mobile terminals

(3)The rise of "mobile wallets" has created new products that integrate mobile phones with bank cards.

(4)Physical branches are dying out, and banks are serving customers in the virtual world.

At present, there is no unified definition of smart banks, but judging from the word "wisdom" itself, it means that in the future banks need to have a "smart" mind, certain "IQ", which causes that the complexity of smart bank construction is higher than the construction of intelligent branches. Intelligent branches are only the front desk of smart banks. The construction of smart banks also requires data analysis behind the scene, risk management, product design, investment and financing planning.

(1)Be able to actively meet customer business needs and interact with customers efficiently.

(2) Be able to use artificial intelligence and other technologies to shape the bank's intelligent decision-making system to improve the bank's "IQ".

(3)Be able to use the internet of things, blockchain and other technologies to build an intelligent ecological chain and realize online and offline smart financial services.

(4)Be able to continuously optimize the bank's operating processes, effectively integrate channels such as mobile banking, online banking, telephone banking, We Chat banking, smart branches, multimedia terminals, and intelligently identify customers and intelligently manage customers to improve service efficiency, lower operating costs, and better the customer service experience.

6.4 Platformization

With the success of e-commerce platforms and social platforms built by Internet companies, "platformization" has become a new profit model different from traditional business models.

Concept: a business model in which a platform enterprise serves as a service platform for bilateral or multilateral markets providing venues and services for interaction between two (or more) specific groups and profiting from them.

(1) Bilateral groups of shopping websites include consumers and online stores. Trilateral groups of search engines include netizens, websites, and advertisers. Multilateral groups of video websites include video viewers, content providers, advertisers, and self-made video users.

(2) Bilateral or multilateral markets can bring "network effects". When more and more people from various groups join the platform, the utility of each person will increase, and then more people will be attracted to enter the platform, and the platform's appeal will increase. The main platform participants form a network overlay effect.

The network overlay effect of the platformization model can help platform companies better assemble users, enhance user stickiness, accumulate data and cross-sell products, which becomes an important basis for commercial banks to intervene in financial technology.

With the rapid spread of mobile Internet, tablet computers and smart phones, the network construction of commercial banks has begun to shift from channel construction to platform construction.

The "Internet + Finance" platform of commercial banks is becoming an open platform with open business, open users, simple processes, and excellent experience to achieve the integration of information, commodities, funds, customers, and business opportunities, and to achieve process embedded financing, standardized network credit , big data trend analysis and other financial services that is in tune with the times.

Commercial banks continue to develop new applications while optimizing their online banking clients side.

(1) Emerging network apps such as mobile banking and Pad Bank have been launched in a row, and new channels such as We Chat Bank and Weibo Bank have gradually gained customer recognition and the customer experience has continued to improve.

(2) Apart from continuously strengthening the innovation and construction of financial service platforms to adapt to the characteristics of people's social life moving to the Internet in the Internet era, services in low relation to financial services such as appointment registration, movie ticket booking and flight booking check-in has also play a crucial

part for banks to enhance customer stickiness and expand financial business.

In addition, large banks have entered the field of e-commerce, e-commerce platforms and housing intermediary platforms have been launched successively, and a new type of banking network platform of "finance + living + commerce" is beginning to take shape.

6.4.1 E-commerce platform

At present, the successful online small loan provides a reference for commercial banks to support small and micro enterprise loans. At the same time, it also poses a huge challenge to the traditional operation and service model of commercial banks. It has filled the commercial bank's small-sum credit vacancy, forced commercial banks to introduce network technologies to address small and micro enterprises' difficulties in borrowing and financing as much as possible.

Learning from successful e-commerce small loan experience, large domestic commercial banks have successively launched their own e-commerce platforms or upgraded existing credit card malls the main purpose of which is to realize precipitation and integration of data resources such as fund, information, and business flow, making up banks shortcomings such as lack of customer transaction, logistics, and social data, and providing banks with financial services such as financing and wealth management based on e-commerce platforms.

Types of domestic mainstream bank e-commerce platforms includes: large multifunctional online mall.

(1) In June 2012, CCB launched "Shanrong Commerce", an e-commerce platform, which is centered on commercial financing. The financial service platform of CCB serves as a platform for commodity wholesale, retail, and housing transactions. Based on this, customers are

provided financial services such as payment settlement, fund trusteeship, installment payments, and loan financing. "Shanrong Commerce" includes two platforms: "personal mall" and "enterprise mall" and a special section. It makes full use of the customer resources and service advantages of CCB to provide a platform of the supply and demand of goods for CCB companies and individual users.

(2) The model adopted by China Construction Bank's "Personal Mall" is to provide products to consumers through joining merchants.

In terms of customer experience there are three modules: shopping mall, merchant center and operation center.

On the consumer side: there are browsing, search and selection, payment purchase, and order management.

When it comes to corporate display: there are reception desk product display, shop management, and operational statistics.

(3)There are also financial services functions for individuals in the mall.

①"Enterprise Mall" is also a B2B platform, which includes three sub-sections: professional market, corporate financing and fund trusteeship. Suppliers engaged in e-commerce can release products, perform online transactions, and conduct supply chain financing on the platform. Buyers can also purchase products in bulk, release purchase information, and apply for financing loans on the platform.

②The special section is the fangetong, which is the advantage of the Construction Bank. This section focuses on the loan business, which is a special business of the Construction Bank compared to other banks' e-commerce. House buyers can click on the house introduction and apply for a home loan directly on the website.

③The Agricultural Bank's e-commerce platform features serving "agriculture, rural areas, and farmers". Based on its E shang guanjia and E nong guanjia, the Agricultural Bank links core enterprises, professional markets, distributors, service points of agriculture, rural areas and farmers with end consumers, takes advantage of offline resources of urban and rural institutional branches to strengthen service to corporate customers, and strives to form business ecosystem in which urban and rural areas, upstream and downstream, and public and private take action altogether.

④ Relatively small-scale stock-based banks frequently use credit card mall upgrades to expand e-commerce. In addition to traditional credit card malls under the credit card column, coupled with many unique service items such as business travel services, wealth management installments, and quota increase, the entire mall and other services are closely surrounding every step of credit card use.

For example, the One Netcom Credit Card column of the China Merchants Bank includes credit card applications, point rewards, wealth management installments, business travel bookings, online malls and other items, especially the "Travel Easy" service launched recently, which is a business travel booking platform introduced for bank credit cards and card holders, serves banks and multiple domestic airlines and hotels, providing flight ticketing and hotel travel booking services for customers

6.4.2 Financial Services Platform

Bank financial service platforms should be customer-centered, integrate banks' online and offline products and services, users and account systems, optimize service processes to form a comprehensive online financial service platform with personalized customization and e-commerce service experience.

Banks can focus on the products and functions of financial service platforms according to the types of customers they serve, such as personal customer financial service platforms and corporate customer financial service platforms. Corporate customers can continue to be subdivided into small business financial service platforms and counterpart financial service platforms.

For individual customers, banks can combine financial services with e-commerce services while focusing on creating mobile and online banking, and give play to the important role of e-commerce platforms to provide various financial products and virtual services.

Compared with traditional e-commerce platforms, banks offer installment services with a number of and a wide range of products, and lower price limits. Almost all products sold in malls can be paid by installment, even if products of more than one hundred yuan are available in bank online malls with a loan.

Many banks have opened "financial halls" or "financial supermarkets" in online shopping malls, and set up multiple financial-related sub-columns such as funds, wealth management products, precious metals, insurance, foreign exchange, personal loans, and futures.

ICBC' rolled out "rong e gou", in addition to similar products in other online malls, and various financial products, such as wealth management products, insurance, precious metal investment, foreign exchange and consumer financial products, and even commodity crowdfunding, housing mortgage and other products.

Banking e-commerce has provided convenient payment methods. (1)Small payments are made directly through bank cards. (2)ICBC's e-shopping mall not only supports traditional bank cards (debit and credit card) for payment, but also supports five special payment methods, including point payment, electronic coupon payment, installment payment, ICBC E Pay and flash purchase payment. (3)Banks such as Pudong Development Bank have also introduced popular shopping methods such as group purchase, limited-time snap-ups, and exemption from handling fees for specific product installments to provide customers with more favorable prices.

The success of the bank's financial service platform is inseparable from whether the bank can build various scenarios that are close to life. In the course of innovation, commercial banks are trying to pinpoint the "scenarios" that can reflect their own advantages.

The Bank of China combined overseas shopping with its inherent cross-border payment settlement and financing business advantages to launch the Bank of China s cross-border e-commerce financial service platform.

Based on the integration and in-depth embedding of the "travel" scene, China Merchants Bank and Didi Chuxing, Nanjing Bank and UBER have reached strategic cooperation, which has new connotations and competitiveness in mobile payment, credit cards, auto finance and even points.

6.4.3 Social life platform

With the popularization of social apps such as Weibo, We Chat, and Baidu Tieba, online social platforms have become an important part in people's daily lives. Commercial banks have also noticed this, and began to provide financial products and services based on social network applications and integrate online social media. And they also introduced online social media into the bank's own platform construction, built a social, living and consumption ecosystem that connects banks, merchants and individual customers, embedded financial products into high-frequency scenarios of customers' daily lives, and enhanced the stickiness of individual customers and merchants, as well as promoted banks transformation of physical branches and targeted marketing of their surroundings by conditional branches.

Some banks have embedded social functions such as contact recording, chat, and messages in their mobile banking apps, trying to build a "financial + social" platform, with the intention of opening the chain of life, information, and financial services, obtaining information on merchants, consumer registration, social interaction, logistics, and transactions to promote the three flows into one(commodity flow, capital flow, and information flow respectively). Through various scenes closely related to life (such as buying movie tickets, booking air tickets, mobile phone recharge, hospital registration inquiry, and merchant discount activities), the habit of consumers using bank mobile APP is formed in which we can find opportunities to provide financial products and services, and promote the transformation and upgrading of bank branches and businesses, laying a foundation for accumulating big data.

(1)Industrial and Commercial Bank of China launched the rongelian instant messaging platform

(2)Bank of China launched Smart E community

(3)Ping An Bank builds a new business social platform in the familiar people business circle of Orange e.com to provide financial services for various scenarios of customer life

(4)Many banks have launched We Chat Bank, which mainly provides basic information services such as account inquiry, credit card services, and notification.

(5)Take ICBC's rongelian for example. The bank claimed to build it into a financial service new model with the goal of an interactive platform for real-time information exchange, business consultation, and communication sharing between the bank and customers, within the bank, and between customers, for social finance and interactive marketing, and introduced a series of new functions such as AA collection, friend transfers, service number voting. Accurate and effective social marketing is carried out through QR code, recommendation code and other methods. As of the end of June 2016, Rongelian has nearly 30 million registered customers.

The three platforms of "finance + life + commerce" have combined the background of banks' opportunities and challenges in financial technology, actively explored the combination of offline and online, created finance of scenes, and truly integrated financial services into every aspect of people's lives.

By creating various scenarios that are close to life and building various platforms, banks have truly takes customer needs as the center, so that customers' financial needs in specific scenarios are met, and financial services are embedded in "clothing, food, shelter, transport, education, entertainment, medicine and life" surrounding daily life of the rank and file, which have changed accordingly. Banks match end-user scenarios requirement with complex and diverse financial services, which has become a reflection of banks' differentiated operations and competitive advantages in the future.

6.5 Bank innovation in the payment field

6.5.1 Bank card service innovation

Faced with the challenge of Alipay and We Chat payment to bank cards, large domestic commercial banks have invested a lot of funds to improve the user experience of bank cards, and main engine-based card simulation technology has become the bank's first choice.

In 2015, Industrial and Commercial Bank of China launched the HCE cloud payment credit card product in cooperation with China

UnionPay and VSA, making it the first commercial bank in Asia to launch this payment product.

(1)Credit card holders do not need to change their mobile phones and SM cards. All they need to do is to make sure that their Android phones have the Near Field Payment (NFC) function, which allows them to log in directly to the ICBC mobile banking interface, click the "Cloud Payment" icon, download HCE payment cloud, bind a credit card and verify activation, through which you can get a virtual credit card, which is similar to a supplementary card bound to a credit card.

(2)When paying offline, the user only needs to turn on the NFC function of the mobile phone and bring the phone close to the POS machine, which enables the payment to be completed instantly

(3)When spending online, the user only needs to bind the HCE cloud payment credit card with ICBCs "ICBC E Pay", and then make the payment according to the interface code.

The entire payment process is very convenient, which can help banks reduce card issuance costs and provide online and offline payment methods. Subsequently, many domestic banks, such as China Construction Bank, Bank of China, Agricultural Bank of China, Pudong Development Bank, Minsheng Bank, and China Guangfa Bank successively launched their own HCE cloud payment services, successfully achieving the convenient service of "mobile phone is credit card".

In recent years, the popularity of financial IC cards has made it to become an important carrier of bank card innovation. As of the end of 2015, nearly 2 billion financial IC cards have been issued nationwide, with an improved acceptance environment and extensive coverage in daily consumption.

(1)In terms of technology, the new-generation financial IC card chip that supports the national secret algorithm already has the conditions for large-scale commercial use, and chip localization has greatly accelerated.

(2)The application scope of financial IC cards is getting wider and wider, and there are extensive application cases in many fields such as social security, public transportation, medical health, tourist attractions, culture and education, and payment of utilities.

In the field of public transportation which frequently uses financial IC card, it has been applied in more than 150 county-level cities across the country for public transportation, rental, railway and other public transportation fields. A bank card replaces the bus IC card, enabling "flash payment" for travel.

At present, the carrier of the financial IC card is the same plastic card as the magnetic stripe card, but in fact, the carrier form of the IC card can be more flexible and diverse, and more based on the customer's individual needs, which integrates the IC card, mobile phone SIM card, and online banking U Shield, or more diverse authentication technologies are adopted to improve the convenience and security of bank cards.

(1)China Construction Bank and Bank of Communications introduced video cards with a LCD display screens and numeric keyboards, which can view account balances and transaction records;

(2)MasterCard Company, an international card organization, applies fingerprint verification technology to credit cards. Users need to press their fingers to verify their identity in the fingerprint recognition area to make the payment, which greatly reduces the risk of unauthorized credit card swiping.

(3) Qianhai, Shenzhen has launched the "Qianhaitong Citizen Card", which is the first citizen card in China to combine biometric technology and intelligent CPU. If it is connected to a financial IC card

in the future, it will further promote the development of bank card technology.

6.5.2 Mobile payment innovation

At present, domestic mobile payment has achieved rapid development. Institutions including commercial banks, UnionPay, third-party payment agencies, and telecom operators are actively promoting payment products such as mobile banking and mobile wallets.

Various banks are actively developing mobile financial applications. At present, state-controlled banks and large stock-based banks have all developed mobile banking applications, and the development rate of city commercial banks is over half.

Although online banking is still the main channel, the proportion of mobile banking users is growing rapidly and the potential for future development is still great.

(1)From the perspective of mobile payment coverage, the top four state-controlled commercial banks rank high, and China Merchants Bank is a leader among stock-based banks.

(2)The investigation shows that the security factor is the main reason why users do not use mobile banking, but once users start using mobile banking, they will transfer inquiry services, simple small-amount businesses, and services that need to go out to handle to it. Customers gradually develop the habit of using mobile banking in preference, promoting the trend of mobile financial services.

From the perspective of business use, mobile banking is more used for remote payment, and users often use mobile banking for account management, financial investment and remittance.

(1)Banks have also made special innovations around mobile banking. Take mobile phone reservations for cash withdrawal for example.

Namely, customers use mobile banking to reserve cardless cash withdrawals. On the same day, they use card reservation codes and withdrawal transaction passwords to implement cardless cash withdrawals on corresponding banks ATMs, which can avoid the risk of the user's bank card information being stolen by criminals on an unattended ATM.

(2) Mobile phone number transfer: Enter the payee name, mobile phone number, payment amount, withdrawal password and other information to transfer to the unit or personal account.

(3) Two-dimensional code transfer. The QR code realizes fund transfer or cash payment between the payer and the payee by generating a bar code within the transfer limit.

(4) Many commercial banks, while expanding their mobile banking clients side, combine We Chat and Alipay public account, and provide services such as credit card repayment and temporary quota adjustment, ATM and business branches check, and bank marketing and promotion activities to extend the bank user base.

(5) Focusing on improving the security and convenience of mobile banking, many domestic and foreign banks are actively cooperating with technology companies to promote the application of Bluetooth and biometrics in mobile payments, and try emerging mobile payment technologies based on wearable devices.

① Fingerprint log and payment launched by China Construction Bank Mobile Bank, guangzizhifu launched by Ping An Bank, Sound waves to pay launched by Bank of China mobile phone client side, facial recognition launched by China Merchants Bank Mobile Bank, and the xiuzizhifu jointly launched by Australia Heritage Bank and VSA. Berkeley Bank plans to apply NFC technology to smart watches and key pendants.

② In the field of near-field payment, banks, mobile operators,

UnionPay, third-party organizations, and mobile phone equipment manufacturers have actively cooperated to jointly promote the development of the near-field payment industry. With the successive entry of Apple and Samsung into the Chinese mobile payment market, NFC technology has gradually become known and has become the main technical means for banks to cope with Alipay and We Chat payment competition. At present, UnionPay is actively expanding the NFC (near field communication) payment scene, and the bank is also vigorously developing corresponding functions in the mobile banking client side.

6.6 Innovative practice of direct selling banks

Direct selling banks were born in economically developed countries such as North America and Europe in the late 1990s, which is a new type of banking operation model that emerged as the times require in the Internet era. Under this business model, banks do not need to set up business branches and physical counters, and do not issue physical bank cards. Customers obtain banking products and services mainly through electronic channels such as computers, email, mobile phones, and telephones. For lack of operating and management costs of the branches, direct selling banks can provide customers with financial services that offer discounts on inventory payment products and on traditional commissions to traditional banks. As the business activities of direct selling banks are mainly carried out through electronic channels and are not restricted by the working hours of employees in physical branches, they can provide customers with round-the-clock and uninterrupted services, which has played a crucial role for commercial banks to meet the challenges of Internet finance.

6.6.1 Features of direct selling banks

1. Targeting middle-income customer groups

Common characteristics of middle-income customer groups:

(1) Pursue discounts, and be sensitive to changes in deposit interest rates.

(2) Be familiar with the Internet, be accustomed to online consumption, and have an open mind about online banking.

(3) Be busy at work and don't like wasting too much time at physical branches.

(4) Don't like over-complex products and have no strong demand for customized products and services.

(5) Aged between 30 and 50 years.

2. "Dematerialization" business model

(1) The main difference between direct selling banks and traditional banks is that they have no physical branches. Today, banks generally carry out multi-channel marketing. Traditional banks widely use telephone banking, online banking, mobile banking and other channels to provide services to customers. But physical branches have always been at the core of traditional bank channel construction.

(2) The direct selling banking model completely shakes off its dependence on physical branches. All customers' banking operations, whether they open accounts or perform transfers, investments, and loans, can be handled directly on the Internet, completely free from restrictions from the space and time.

(3) Since there is no branch, if the customer wants to withdraw cash, he can transfer the money in the direct selling bank account to his own corresponding account in another bank for free.

(4) Of course, some direct selling banks will also set up some physical branches to support their online business. For example, ING

Direct, which has been very successful, has set up a customer information center, but its main function is to promote the brand of the bank and to help customers understand the use of online or telephone banks. It generally does not handle specific business.

3.Does not pursue personalization of products and services

(1)Affected by its customer positioning, direct selling banks do not seek to become comprehensive banks, nor do they aim to provide complex and diverse products. Their products are generally demand and fixed deposits, transfers, remittances, online payments, mortgage loans, and financial investment.

(2)There are also fewer types of products for customers to choose from under each category. They do not provide personalized and customized products and services, and do not pursue everything. Instead, they provide customers with the most commonly used products at a price at a sharp discount, making customers less troubled when choosing products.

4.Preferential prices

Direct selling banks often share the money saved without setting up physical branches with customers, attract customers with preferential prices, and earn profits with a strategy of small profits but quick turnover.

(1)Pay higher interest rates on customers' savings deposits, usually more than twice that of traditional physical banks.

(2) Generally do not charge account management fees or online banking annual fees.

(3)Provide gifts for new customers or free cross-border credit card cash withdrawal.

(4)Encourage public praise marketing. Old customers will receive points or gifts as a reward after successfully recommending new customers to open an account.

5.Simplified transaction processes

(1)Direct selling bank transactions are simpler and more convenient than traditional banks. Banks need to design simple covers that allow customers to complete operations through self-service channels.

(2)Take the opening of a savings account for example. Customers can complete the application by entering information such as name, gender, ID number, and other bank accounts online, saving the time cost of opening an account at a physical branch.

6.6.2 Model of direct selling banks

Direct selling banks are not new. The development of information technology and changes in customer behavior are the main factors affecting the business model of direct selling banks.

The operating models of direct selling banks in foreign countries mainly include pure online banking models, global direct selling banks, direct selling banks as sub-brands, and direct selling banks as business units.

The three main operating models of direct selling banks in China includes:

1.Pure online model

(1)This is a model that is closest to the definition of direct selling banks. Without physical branches, the bank only uses electronic channels such as telephone, online and mobile banking to provide customers with financial services. All financial services of customers can be obtained through direct selling bank mobile phone apps, We Chat Bank or official website operation.

(2)Seen from the current situations, most direct selling banks in China use pure online models, like Industrial Bank, Jiangsu Bank, and

Xiaoma Bank. Customers who bind their bank account or another bank account to a direct selling bank account can enjoy its services and products. When cash withdrawal is needed, the funds in the bank account are transferred to the physical bank card. Cash from the counter or ATM of the physical card bank is withdrew.

2.Online + offline direct selling store model

(1)The method combining online and offline is adopted, including both online channels consisting of electronic channels such as official websites and mobile phone APPs, and offline channels consisting of multiple self-service devices and physical stores.

(2)The physical store may be a convenience store set up by a direct selling bank alone, or may be based on the business branches of the parent bank. The former, such as the Bank of Beijing Direct Selling Bank, has now opened direct sales stores in Beijing, Jinan, Nanjing, Xi'an and other places, placing various self-service equipment such as ATMs, self-service payment terminals, and smart banking machines, supplemented by various self-service operation channels such as online, telephone, We Chat and mobile bank. Bohai Bank's Haoetong is a classic example.

(3)The combination of online and offline channels builds a three-dimensional service system that can meet the multi-level and diversified financial needs of different customers.

3.Online + Internet Business Model

Direct selling banks build an integrated online platform, and cooperates with third-party Internet companies to develop customers and products through data information sharing, like Bank of Beijing Direct Selling Bank and 360 Company, Minsheng Bank and Alibaba, Guiyang Bank Direct Selling Bank and JUSFOUN big data company.

(1)Take the Bank of Beijing Direct Selling Bank for example. The cooperation between Bank of Beijing and Qihoo 360 Technology mainly intends to create a network security system for direct selling banks. Both parties will cooperate in the fields of coordinated control of Internet financial risks, data slip prevention, security services, and Internet finance to create an authoritative and secure Internet financial services platforms.

(2) The cooperation between Minsheng Bank and Alibaba focuses more on the use of big data for customer and product development. Minsheng Bank can take advantage of Alibaba's advantages in data analysis and network traffic to conduct business and sell financial products on the Alibaba e-commerce platform.

6.6.3 Development of direct selling banks in China

The popularity of the Internet and e-commerce creates a platform and carrier for the development of direct selling banks.

6.6.3.1 Development of domestic direct selling banks

On September 18, 2013, Bank of Beijing announced the cooperation with Dutch ING Group to provide direct selling banking services, which made direct selling banks emerge in China.

On February 28, 2014, the direct selling bank of Minsheng Bank went online, which triggered a boom in the development of domestic direct selling banks.

According to incomplete statistics, as of the end of 2015, nearly 50 banks in China set up direct selling banks, including large state-owned holding banks, such as the rongehang of Industrial and Commercial Bank of China, and national stock-based banks, such as Industrial Bank Direct Selling Bank, Huaxia Bank Direct Selling Bank, and SPDB (shanghai pu dong development bank) Direct Selling Bank. More are established by local commercial banks, such as Chongqing Bank Direct Selling Bank, Bank of Beijing Direct Selling Bank, and Baoshang Bank Xiaoma Bank.

The main reason for this layout is the lack of physical branches of local banks and stock-based banks. The development of direct selling banks is an important way for them to respond to the interest rate marketization and Internet financial challenges and increase customers.

The business of domestic direct selling banks is mainly based on deposits and investment and wealth management. Some banks have embedded concepts such as peer-to-peer lending (P2P) credit investment, financial search, and cross-border e-commerce financing based on currency fund products or deposits, thereby presenting business diversification.

In 2015, the direct banking model showed two major characteristics.

(1)Graft off-site account opening products.

The biggest highlight of direct selling banks is the cross-validation of mobile phone numbers, ID numbers and bank card numbers, thereby achieving diversified off-site account opening

The shortcomings are that each is still at the early stage of exploration, each direct selling bank has a single style, and the products and functions are not enough and the same as others. Most direct selling bank accounts are weak real-name electronic accounts, with certain limited functions and permissions.

(2)Incorporate the concept of Internet cross-border development.

As more and more banks enter this area, direct selling banks have gradually expanded their product sources and introduced the concept of cross-border Internet finance in their business models. For example, the "integrated intelligent financial management platform" will gradually transfer traditional financial management services online, while adding stock funds, insurance, gold, and art investment to the financial management platform.

6.6.3.2 Typical examples of direct selling banks at home and abroad

1.ING Direct

ING Direct is a direct selling bank established by International Nederlanden Group in Canada in 1997. After its success, Internationale Nederlanden Group quickly established similar institutions in the United States, Spain, France, Germany, the United Kingdom and other countries, focusing on overseas retail banking business, which has now become a model for direct selling banking.

ING Direct's business model is to provide customers with basic financial products through electronic channels such as telephone and Internet. Its business includes current accounts, savings accounts, personal mortgage loans, credit cards, and intermediate services. ING Directs principles of "simple" and "small profits but quick turnover" in the operation of direct selling banks are important reasons for its success.

(1)Accurate customer positioning

ING Direct emphasizes oneness when identifying target customers. The customer group has the following characteristics:

①The middle income class, and pay much attention to the growth of interest income

②Use traditional bank branches not frequently and like simplified transaction procedures

③Receive good education, and have habits of internet consumption and the use of Internet and telephone banking

④Aged between 30 and 50 years old.

For this reason, unlike the traditional "Paretos principles", ING Direct does not intend to attract the richest customers. Instead, it strives to provide the most needed products to customers with homogeneity, and attracts and retains customers with simple, low-cost products.

(2)Product positioning is "simple"

The important point of online marketing is to standardize the product as much as possible to reduce the customer's dependence on the account manager and the number of telephone banking services. Therefore, when designing banking products, ING Direct not only made the product structure simple and easy to understand, but also kept the company's comparative advantage from the perspective of cost control.

ING Direct mainly has four strategies in terms of products:

Limited choice: The direct sales channel offers a limited variety of products, which are concentrated in savings and some loan, making it easy for customers to make quick choices.

Direct selling bank accounts are linked to others, and customers can obtain funds from their current accounts in other banks.

"Self-service" products that focus on full network operation. Customers can operate independently through the network.

There is no minimum deposit requirement, which reduces the cost burden on customers to purchase products.

(3)Supporting measures and support services

①"Online + Offline" integrated marketing with different emphasis

Based on a survey of the development of the local banking industry, ING Direct taps into the resources of the entire group to develop direct selling bank products that meet the demands of the target customers, and uses the local multi-probe network that is well-known to promote the products and advantages of direct selling banks.

In order to enhance customer trust and reduce the distance between customers and banks, ING Direct opened online cafes in cities with denser customers to provide the brand with a real offline presence and that consumers can feel.

Customers and potential customers can drink coffee, surf the internet and chat here. Cafe clerks are financial consultants trained by banks. When customers need them, they can provide them with relevant financial service advice in simple language. However, they do not deal directly with customers.

②Convenient network services and cross-market financial services

To allow customers to complete transactions via the Internet or phone in the shortest time and reduce customer time costs, banks strive to make the interface simple, friendly and process-oriented.

In addition to providing traditional banking products, ING Direct also provides customers with a variety of financial products across markets, such as mortgages, common funds, annuities and life insurance. Since direct selling banks do not have branches and ATMs, customers need to deposit and withdraw cash from the bank branches associated with their ING Direct accounts. Throughout the process, ING Direct provides free services.

③Stable background system and sound call center system

Information technology is extremely important to the operation of direct selling banks. ING Direct has accumulated rich background system construction experience since the operation of the first direct selling bank in Canada. Through continuous improvement and upgrade, the security and stability of the background system are continuously improved.

In order to win customers' trust and communicate with customers without obstacles, ING Direct arms call centers composed of local personnel around the world. When a customer encounters a problem, he can get a reply through the call center to solve the problem.

2.First Direct

First Direct was founded by British Midland Bank in 1989. In 1992, the HSBC acquired Midland Bank, so that First Direct became part of HSBC, a subsidiary of the HSBC Group.

Similar to ING Direct, First Direct, which is characterized by unique brand positioning, more interaction with customers, and multiple marketing methods, is also a direct selling bank with precise positioning of its target customers and their financial products.

(1)Unique brand positioning

First Direct emphasizes the differences between traditional bank and itself when promoting its brand. Personality-focused promotional strategies appeal greatly to young people, which also lay the foundation for First Direct to win future potential customers.

(2)More interaction with customers

①First Direct has set up a website called First Direct Lab, which is designed for customers to put forward any ideas and suggestions about it, to participate in First Direct questionnaires, to comment on a certain new product or to participate in the design of a product that is being developed, which enables the bank to get closer to customers, know what their customers want, include customer needs into products and services, and improve quality and service levels of bank products.

②In addition, this approach can also make bank customers feel valued. By interacting with customers, it allows them to participate in the bank's product design and service improvement, increasing customers sense of participation, identity, and brand loyalty.

(3)New marketing methods

In order to attract customers to open an account and transfer funds to a new account, First Direct has adopted a variety of novel marketing methods.

For example, First Direct has launched an event called "Switch Guarantee", which includes: Account opening bonus: If a new customer transfers 1,000 pounds to a new account every month for three consecutive months, 100 pounds of funds and 250 pounds of interest-free overdraft will be rewarded; satisfaction promise: If the customer transfers to the new account for 1,000 per month for 6 consecutive months, and there is dissatisfaction in the next 6 months, First Direct will compensate the client for 100 and help him or her cancel the account.

(4)Call center with purely manual service

The design of First Direct's call center is very thoughtful. Unlike other call centers, which must choose multiple times before they can access the human service, customers call the call center and the phone directly accesses the human service to help answer customer questions, simplifying the service process to the greatest extent, and receiving praise from customers.

(5)First Direct's charging strategy

Since there is no need to pay high costs of branches and labor costs, most direct selling banks share the benefits of cost savings with customers, pay customers higher deposit interest rates or require lower loan interest rates, and earn profits by small profits and more sales, and generally charge less service fees.

First Direct's approach is slightly different. Banks began charging bank service fees in November 2006 at 10 per month. The above fees will be waived when the customer meets certain conditions like new customers within six months of opening an account, customers who have deposited at least 1,000 pounds per month, customers with an average monthly balance greater than 1,000 pounds, or customers who hold certain products of the bank.

3.Direct selling bank of Bank of Beijing

On September 18, 2013, Bank of Beijing announced the launch of a direct selling bank service model in cooperation with Internationale Nederlanden Group, which becomes the first direct selling banking in the Chinese market.

Unlike ING Direct's pure online operation model, Bank of Beijing Direct Selling Bank adopts a service model integrated online and offline. The former is composed of a variety of electronic services such as an integrated Internet marketing platform, online banking, mobile banking, and video conversations. The latter is composed of a variety of self-service terminals such as a convenient direct selling store offline, and VTM (video teller machine), ATM, CRS (cash recycling system) and self-service payment terminals as well as various self-service operation channels such as online banking and telephone banking.

Bank of Beijing has established a number of direct selling branches in Beijing, Xi'an, and Jinan. Through the "Internet platform + direct selling branch" approach, Bank of Beijing integrates offline and online, which is more like a financial convenience store that combines virtual and reality to meet the financial needs of customers in three-dimensional, diverse, and different scenarios.

Starting from multiple levels such as customer positioning, product design, system construction and process control, the bank provides retail customers and small and micro enterprises with uninterrupted services around the clock which is a meaningful attempt.

4.Minsheng Bank Direct Selling Bank

On February 28, 2014, the direct selling bank of Minsheng Bank was officially launched.

Minsheng Bank's direct selling bank mainly develops customers through Internet channels, which has the characteristics of clear-cut banks' customers and simple products. In response to the customer's positioning of "busy, trendy, and sophisticated", banking products are prominently simple and affordable, and the bank launched a wealth management product "Ruyibao" and a savings product "Save As You Want", and subsequently launched several similar products.

In terms of channel construction, Minsheng Bank focuses on providing customers with websites, mobile banking and We Chat banking that are easy to operate.

Compared with mobile banking and third-party payment, Minsheng Bank Direct Selling Bank has two major advantages:

(1)Direct selling banks have achieved the characteristics of off-site account opening. Non-Minsheng Bank customers can open an account in Minsheng Bank Direct Selling Bank by binding other bank cards and transfer funds to a new account. Direct selling banks established by many banks now adopt this method.

(2) Compared with third-party payment, Minsheng Bank Direct Selling Bank functions fully as a bank account. Its virtual account is positioned as a personal settlement account, with complete deposit and loan functions which cannot be achieved by third-party payments alone.

6.7 Relationship between blockchain and banks

6.7.1 The impact of blockchain on banks

Blockchain technology is extremely disruptive to banks, which is mainly reflected in the following two aspects:

1.Blockchain technology disrupts lowest technology

With the continuous emergence of new technologies, the business model of banks has been continuously making progress(see Figure 1-1). For example, the application of the cloud platform system has changed the banking industry's business processing and infrastructure deployment model, which has greatly reduced operating costs. The concept of big data risk control has completely changed the risk control model that was previously judged by experience. Banks have begun to adopt risk control models that enables machine learning, greatly improving audit efficiency. However, the above Internet technologies have only changed the upper-layer applications and business processes in the financial field, and have not changed the underlying logic and related technologies under the banking business model. However, the emergence of blockchain technology will completely subvert the underlying technical foundation of the bank's business model, especially the way of information interaction between its systems and the mode of transaction settlement. If the blockchain is applied to a bank, then the bank can update the ledger information when the transaction is made. All transactions are liquidated at the moment they are made. After adopting the blockchain technology, all the banks' systems will use the same technology protocol, which will greatly reduce the compatibility risk when information is exchanged between systems. In addition, because the blockchain has a time stamp, once the transaction rules between the participants are written into the blockchain according to the rules of the agreement, it will become a standard and cannot be tampered with.

2.Promoters of business system innovation

The emergence of blockchain technology has changed the institutional basis of the current business model and the relationship between all participants under this model to some extent. The establishment of the existing financial system cannot be separated from three basic institutional frameworks: commercial trust relies on legal provisions; asset transfer transactions are guaranteed by independent third parties as credit intermediaries; transaction settlement and clearing are processed by centralized clearing institutions. However, the advent of blockchain technology will subvert these institutional foundations and business processes that people take for granted. Facing this change, financial intermediaries under the traditional institutional framework should adjust their roles in a timely manner, such as Visa, a payment organization that pays for intermediary services, and Nasdaq, a securities issuance and transaction market platform, which have found that blockchain technology, in the future, will change their business value, so it adopts a positive attitude to welcome technological innovation, cooperate with Chain (American blockchain technology start-up), and invest funds in areas where blockchain technology can be applied.

For banks, whether they will be the beneficiaries or subverted parties in this new technological innovation depends to some extent on their attitudes towards blockchain technology. Banks should clearly recognize their role in the future business landscape. They must not just act as credit intermediaries that charge interest margins and transaction costs. Instead, they need to embrace new technologies in positive attitudes, and improve their own financial services capabilities by blockchain technology, which can be applied to different businesses of banks, including payment settlement, bill circulation, supply chain finance, and securities issuance and transaction, which will benefit all transaction participants, including banks, bank customers, and bank cooperators (such as platform enterprises).

The application of blockchain technology will break the current efficiency bottlenecks, transaction delays, fraud and operational risks in various financial service processes. For example, the manual operation, manual verification and approval in the existing process will be transformed into automated processing, and the paper contract industry will be replaced by smart contracts, thereby reducing systemic risks in the transaction processing link. According to relevant statistics, the blockchain technology can save 40% of transaction costs in cross-border payment and settlement business transaction processes.

6.7.2 Combination of bank business and blockchain

6.7.2.1 Digital currency

The emergence and development of Bitcoin and other digital currencies has overturned peoples concept of money and gradually changed the way people use it. With the development of human business behaviors and society, the currency used for transaction has evolved from physical items to gold and silver to the credit currency used at present. Now, electronic finance and e-commerce have found their way into people's lives, because digital currencies are secure, convenient, and has a low transaction cost, which is obviously more suitable for network transactions. It has replaced the status of physical currency to some extent.

Bitcoin is a good example. European and American countries have accepted this type of digital currency to some extent, allowing it to be used to pay for goods, and Bitcoin debit cards, ATMs and other spin-offs have also appeared on the market. And, some institutions have established transaction platforms that allow digital currencies and legal currencies to circulate freely. For example, Coin Base, the Bitcoin transaction platform in the United States, and OK Coin, the Chinese transaction platform, support circulation transactions between them.

In addition, many countries have also begun to try to issue digital currencies. Both Ecuador and Tunisia used blockchain technology to issue digital currency under the control of the country which can be used in the purchase and sale of goods, and payment of utility bills.

At the same time, Australia, Russia, Sweden and other countries have also begun to explore the feasibility of issuing digital currencies. The British Central Bank has commissioned the University of London to design a digital currency called RS Coin and put it into trials. In January 2016, the People's Bank of China also held a digital currency seminar, which proposed to seek the early issuance of digital currencies managed by the central bank.

Central banks of all countries pay attention to digital currencies because of the obvious advantages of digital currencies over physical cash. It can make transaction payment more convenient, reduce the cost of traditional currency issuance and circulation, and also record the transaction process through the network, prevent illegal crimes such as money laundering and tax evasion, and improve the central bank's ability to control currency supply and circulation. At the same time, when blockchain technology is applied to digital currencies, the security of funds and information will be guaranteed more rigorously than ever.

6.7.2.2 Cross-border payment and settlement

The above case of Ripple using the blockchain to establish a global distributed clearing and settlement system has already mentioned the reform of the blockchain to the banking industry in the field of cross-border payment and settlement. After the adoption of blockchain technology, transactions between banks will cancel the intermediaries acted by third-party financial institutions, and directly implement the point-to-point payment model, thereby eliminating hidden costs, and bringing advantages of payment at any time, real-time arrival and fast withdrawal. According to James OMcKinsey's calculations, after blockchain technology is applied to B2B cross-border payment and settlement business, the cost of each transaction will decrease from ＄26 to 15.

6.7.2.3 Bills and supply chain finance

At present, there is a third-party role in bill transactions to increase the credibility of the bill transaction process. For example, when exchanging paper bills, the trust is based on the authenticity of the bills; electronic bills rely on the inspection certificate of the Central Bank's ECDS system. Blockchain technology will replace the role of the original intermediary. Buyers and sellers can directly make point-to-point transactions, without the need for physical bills and credit enhancement links that EXDS systems act as.

Blockchain can also be applied to supply chain finance. Existing supply chain finance uses paper to complete operations. Blockchain can help digitize this process. Decentralized ledger will replace the existing system, all participating parties (including suppliers, sellers, and banks) use this ledger to make transactions and store information, which can not only increase efficiency, but also reduce problems caused by manual operations.

According to James OMcKinsey's calculations, after blockchain technology is applied to the supply chain finance business, a large-scale bank can reduce operating costs of approximately ＄ 13.5 billion to 15 billion a year, and risk costs of ＄ 1.1 billion to 1.6 billion. It can also reduce capital costs of approximately ＄ 1.1 billion to 1.3 billion and operating costs of ＄ 1.6 billion to 2.1 billion between buyers and sellers.

Blockchain technology can effectively prevent fraud, because all customer information and transaction records are stored on the blockchain, and the transaction and customer information of the blockchain are updated in real time, which will be automatically encrypted, associated and shared. Banks can judge which transactions are abnormal by analyzing and monitoring shared information, thereby preventing fraud. At present, some companies have begun to design blockchain-based systems for banks. For example, Chainalysis, a start-up company with the intention of combating anti-fraud and digital currency money laundering, began to design blockchain analysis monitoring system to help banks conduct anti-money laundering and fraud by monitoring public ledger.

Chapter 7 Application and Development of the Insurance Industry

Considering the current development of the insurance industry, the development and application of a series of new technologies and new products such as the Internet, big data, cloud computing, blockchain, internet of things, connected cars, and wearable devices have changed the insurance industry from multiple dimensions such as operation ideas, commercial models, technical means, sales channels, internal management, making Fintech the core driving force leading the transformation and upgrading of the insurance industry and the optimization of the industry's development environment.

7.1 Internet technology brings a disruptive revolution to the business model of the insurance industry

7.1.1 The Impact of Internet technology on the development of China's insurance industry

Internet technology has had a profound impact on the competitive landscape of the insurance market: the traditional large and medium-sized insurance industry has deeply broadened Internet channels through the establishment of official websites and e-commerce companies. Some small and medium-sized insurance companies have taken advantage of new technologies to enter the Internet insurance market, with the intention of "overtaking in curve"; large Internet companies that have "snooped" on traditional financial markets for a long time have begun to arrange the insurance market; the third-party operating entities such as insurance intermediaries have also hit the Internet insurance market, and competition has intensified.

Internet insurance premiums have increased exponentially: Internet insurance premiums has increased by 69 times to 9.3% in scale, up from 1.7% of the total premium in 2013, which has become one of the important factors driving the growth of premiums.

Internet insurance business entities continue to expand: Internet giants such as Tencent, Alibaba and China Ping An lay out a Internet of Number insurance market; Baidu, HillHouse Capital and Allianz have jointly established Baian Insurance; Taikang Online, yiyan Online, and Anxin Property and other Internet insurance companies have been established one after another.

The number of Internet insurance customers and social attention have also increased significantly: With the rapid development of Internet insurance, social capital has also begun to favor Internet insurance companies.

7.1.2 Development trend of Internet technology in insurance industry

1.The Internet will continue to expand the insurance product innovation space and insurance market scope

The rapid popularization of the Internet has turned the shangwang era into the online era. The consumption and payment of the public has shifted rapidly, giving insurance companies a greater space for product innovation, and increasing the capacities of leadership and creation of customer demands.

The development of the Internet has enabled smart mobile terminals to quickly replace traditional PC terminals, becoming the main channel for the public to connect the Internet. As a result, consumer behaviors have broken time and geographical restrictions. Customers can use smart mobile terminals to be online in real time, and make purchases and payments anytime and anywhere. The risks contained in Internet consumption and online payment can produce new insurance needs, which will open up new markets for the insurance industry.

In the future, there will be a large number of innovative insurance products such as "refund shipping insurance" that protect Internet consumption and payment conducts.

2. The Internet will help insurance to be scenarios, so that more fragmented insurance needs will be met

In the Internet era, various high-frequent and fragmented demands are emerging, and being scenario-based is an effective way to meet these needs.

The insurance demand generated by offline scenarios has stimulated the development of traditional insurance products, and the popularity of the Internet has gradually moved many offline scenarios online. The emergence of online scenarios has created an opportunity for the emergence of Internet insurance products.

In the future, insurance companies will develop innovative insurance products which can be embedded in the Internet ecosystem and knit insurance services seamlessly into the Internet consumption purchase, payment, and logistics, reducing costs without affecting the user experience to meet customers' high-frequent, fragmented insurance needs.

3. The Internet has increased the sales channels of insurance prod-

ucts, which will further broaden the insurance service rate space

The Internet has expanded insurance sales channels, and insurance companies can overcome geographical restrictions and provide products and services to customers in different regions anytime and anywhere through the Internet.

In the future, sales of insurance products through Internet channels will enable the insurance industry to further shake off the shackles of the agent system in traditional marketing systems and reduce sales costs.

4.The Internet will update the service model of the insurance industry at length

The development of Internet technology has enabled insurance services to break time and geographical restrictions, and created unlimited possibilities for the innovation of insurance service models.

Getting customers' physical condition information through wearable devices and mobile phone health monitoring software allows insurance companies to provide personalized health risk management solutions at any time; real-time management and control of insured property through the internet of things terminal enable insurance companies to manage the property they promise to protect in a more refined and dynamic way, and provide more refined and personalized loss prevention and reduction solutions; obtaining driving behavior information and vehicle, road state and accident information through connected cars can innovate product pricing models and provide driving behavior management, active rescue and other services.

5.The in-depth application of the Internet will further highlight the "customer-centered" concept

The Internet makes customers no longer passively receive information by insurance companies, customer demands become the driving force behind the emergence of new insurance products, and their behavior data becomes the basis for insurance product design, which also means that customers can turn passive into active and participate in the whole process of insurance product design and service.

In this process, big data such as customer behavior data, consumption habits, and payment preferences will gradually become the core resources for insurance companies to compete.

The Internet can not only enable customers to choose insurance products suitable for their own needs more freely, but also make it easier and more convenient for customers to compare and choose between different insurance companies and products. Insurance companies should actively follow this development trend, make the premiums more transparent, and keep the rights and interests more clearly, which can not only attract more customers, but also significantly lower the cash surrender rate of insurance sales.

6.With the help of Internet technology, the operation and management of insurance companies will be continuously improved

Internet technology can improve the speed and ability of insurance companies to respond to the market, grasp new developments in the insurance market in a timely manner, tap potential customer groups, discover various innovative products on the market, and adopt appropriate business strategies at any time.

Internet technology will enable the core operating processes and customer service of insurance companies to be networked and self-serviced, improve the efficiency of insurance companies' handling of business, reduce costs, improve management levels, and increase customer satisfaction.

Internet technology enables insurance companies to directly face customers without agency companies and agents, which significantly reduces sales and management costs.

7.Under the influence of Internet technology, the insurance industry will pay more attention to protection of customer rights and information disclosure

Insurance is no longer traditional products that can only guarantee life, old age, sickness, death, and disability, but has developed into various fields that are closely related to customers' daily life, work, and consumption behaviors. There is huge room for innovation in the form, variety, coverage, and degree of insurance products

However, the level of consumer knowledge lags behind the innovation level of Internet insurance causes the low overall level of knowledge of financial consumers in China, which may trigger a series of problems such as damage to consumer rights and interests, and low recognition of innovative insurance products. Therefore, how to raise consumer awareness, increase their ability to choose insurance products and identify and prevent risks are undoubtedly an inevitable important issue for the healthy development of the insurance industry in the future.

Open and transparent information transmission is the core advantage of the Internet and an important guarantee for the sustainable and healthy development of Internet insurance.

While the marketization of the insurance industry is increasing, Internet technology can help insurance companies refine the information disclosure rules of Internet insurance products, and clearly reveal requirements in terms of insurance liabilities, notification obligations, exemption clauses, and rights and obligations of cancellation of insurance, thereby preventing sales from being misleading.

7.2 Big data technology helps promote comprehensive upgrading of the insurance industry

The application of big data and other technologies may fundamentally change the rules and business models of the financial industry, including the insurance industry.

The insurance industry is born with a big data gene, which is, in essence, an industry that manages risks through data collection, analysis, and forecasting.

At present, the big data strategy has become national, marking the dawn of China's big data era. Big data technology will upgrade and transform insurance industry from the business philosophy, business model, product design, management process.

In the future, data will become the core resource of the insurance industry. At the same time, data mining, analysis, and application capabilities will become the core competitiveness of the insurance industry.

7.2.1 Features of big data technology applied in the insurance industry

In the future, the insurance industry's decisions will all be based on data. Actuarial modeling, risk control, product R&D, product pricing, and marketing will all rely on data to analyze results.

The continuous growth of the insurance business, the expansion of the market scope, and the increasing diversification of insurance products have dramatically expanded the data of the insurance industry. Basic customer information (identity information, policy information, image information) ,credit information, payment preferences, web browsing records, e-commerce transaction records and other unstructured data will affect the degree of customer risk and also generate new insurance needs.

The main characteristics of big data technology applied in the insurance industry:

1. increased data complexity will make unstructured data become mainstream

Analyzing China's Internet penetration and utilization rate, in the future, unstructured data will completely replace structured data, becoming the main data source for the insurance industry.

The insurance industry should follow the trend of technological development, invest more in R&D of big data technologies, improve the ability of insurance companies to collect, store, analyze and predict data, get value from unstructured data, and continuously optimize, based on better serving customers, enterprise management processes, forming the core competitiveness of "big data drive".

2. The insurance industry begins to pay more attention to the value of big data, and insurance companies have a solid foundation for big data analysis

Major domestic insurance companies have begun to attach importance to the development of big data technologies, formulate development strategies for informatization and big data construction, and make big data technologies the key to product pricing and marketing. They also advocate continuously accumulating customer data through social software and network platforms, analyze user data through big data technology, discover value and forecast, improve insurance product pricing mechanism, design personalized insurance products, and accurately grasp customer insurance needs, and promote them to customers precisely.

Attaching importance to accumulating data on the intra-company operations, and using financial statements, human resource changes, product sales, insurance claims, and market response as the basis for monitoring the company's operating status, judging market trends, and adjusting business strategies, as well as create a big data basis for insurance companies to reshape their business model and upgrades their internal management processes.

At present, most domestic insurance companies use big data technologies to varying degrees in terms of actuarial model structure, product pricing, and insurance claims. As a result, they have established information-based mechanisms such as business analysis systems, finance analysis systems, call centers, and backup information centers, providing effective data and technical support for the development of insurance business.

3. Obviously insufficient breadth and depth of big data technology applications contribute to further developed and utilized emerging technologies

There are still few cases of accurately designing products to meet customer needs, and the problem of homogenization of insurance products still exists.

The insurance industry has not yet established a customer credit database, which failed to make joint analysis of customer insurance data and other financial data.

Financial big data is really taken advantage of; giving full play to guarantee risk of insurance, serving social and economic development, and addressing people's livelihood needs to be strengthened; some emerging technologies based on big data have not been widely used in the insurance industry.

4. The demand for big data talents is growing, but the construction of professional big data talent teams is slightly behind

At present, the insurance industry has accumulated a considerable number of specialized data analysis talents in actuarial modeling, risk management and control, and product pricing. These talents constitute the talent team for current insurance companies to build big data platforms, but talents who have both Internet thinking and big data thinking and are familiar with the insurance industry's business processes and business models are few, the shortage of whom stands in the way on the development of big data strategies for insurance companies.

7.2.2 The development trend of the application of big data technology in the insurance industry

1. The status of data as the "core asset" of the insurance industry will be further strengthened

In the era of big data, data will become the key to the core competitiveness of the industry. For insurance companies, data is the core asset, and data analysis capabilities are the core competitiveness.

Data collection not only needs to use the Internet to obtain customer behavior data, but also acquire potential customer behavior data to prepare for future market expansion and new market demand; from the perspective of data application, insurance companies should use big data analysis capabilities to fully know customer needs, understand the characteristics and needs of each customer through data collection, providing them with more personalized and customized services and products.

Under the influence of the rapid development of Internet information technology, decentralization, diversification, and miniaturization have become the mainstream development of mobile terminals. Customers may use different payment methods to use different mobile terminals for consumption anytime and anywhere. As a result, a large number of irregular and fragmented consumer information is formed, which poses a huge challenge to the ability of insurance companies to collect, integrate, process, and analyze information, and also places extremely high demands on the complex and flexible operating capabilities of insurance companies.

2.Big data technology can help the insurance industry achieve precise marketing

The in-depth application of big data technology greatly improves the ability of insurance companies to obtain and deeply dig data, making customer behavior data gradually become available, analyzable, and predictable. Customer responses to insurance products will also be obtained by insurance companies in a timely manner, which has a strong impact on the traditional marketing system of insurance companies, and makes it possible for insurance sales to pass through the intermediateagents.

How to use big data technology to hit customers' "pain points" and achieve accurate marketing and how to use the right platform and promote the right insurance products to the right customers at the right time has become the main direction for insurance companies to reshape the marketing system in the era of big data.

3.Big data technology will further expand the insurance market and open up a new "blue ocean" market

With the changes in the economic situation and the development of marketization, there will be a large number of sub-sectors in the insurance market. Due to the constraints of the traditional marketing system, traditional insurance companies have no time to deal with each of the sub-sectors in the process of marketization. Or diseconomies of scale contributes to limited segmentation of customers and markets. Or it can not promise to cover every segmented area, thus forming a market gap.

In the future, insurance companies will be able to make use of the advantages of big data technology to achieve in-depth mining of original customer resources, while also covering customers in different regions and industries, providing products and services of traditional dis-economies of scale, occupying the broad "blue ocean market", gaining more customer resources and their behavioral data, forming a virtuous circle of development.

Big data technology provides data basis for aiming at customers' needs, and personalized, customized and differentiated insurance products; with the in-depth application of big data technology, insurance companies can improve their abilities about risk pricing and risk management, and can include risks they previously are unable to or have difficulty in effectively managing into the capabilities of insurance companies.

4.Big data technology will innovate risk management technology in the insurance industry

In terms of connected cars, insurance companies can know the health information and the driving habits of the insured, the real-time status of the vehicle, and the risk status of the roads where the vehicle is often driven. It can provide personalized risk management services on the basis of different risk levels of customers to achieve risk reduction management.

In terms of medical insurance, insurance companies can obtain and monitor the health status of customers in real time through wearable devices. Not only can they tailor insurance solutions for customers, but also they can make alarms and send rescue information when customer health data is abnormal to reduce risk losses. In addition, insurance companies can also strengthen business risk management and improve anti-fraud technology through big data technologies.

5.Big data technology will help optimize the organization and management of insurance companies

Judging from the nature of the industry, insurance is an industry that operates risks. Whether it can succeed in managing depends on the professionalism of the insurance company's risk management technology. In the future, the rapid development of big data technology will not only enable insurance companies to change their marketing and service methods, but also create a driving force for insurance companies to reshape their own organizational structures and management systems, making it possible for insurance companies to rebuild the enterprise information management system.

Insurance companies should employ big data technology into key links and processes of insurance company operations, optimize business, management, information, customer service, and decision support systems, and make big data technologies play an active role in enterprise management and operations, information construction and maintenance, customer service and new product development.

The application of big data technology in the insurance industry can form a competitive advantage in customer big data analysis, which is also of great significance to the long-term stable development of insurance companies; it will also continue to promote the transparency of insurance companies' insurance information, which is conducive to the establishment of an image of integrity by insurance companies.

7.3 Cloud computing technology is an accelerator that promotes innovation and development of the insurance industry

Computing is a new computing model that breaks the traditional main machine frame model and implements a layered and distributed structure of the system, that is, to have access to customized and shared resource pools in a convenient, and low-cost manner through the network at any time and be paid based on times.

7.3.1 The development trend of cloud computing technology applied in the insurance industry

1.Cloud computing technology will help insurance companies with their business innovation

Insurance companies can use cloud computing technology to create an "insurance cloud" tailored to the enterprise, and develop insurance core business, financial and process management modules in the cloud, through which customers can complete insurance and claims settlement and other insurance services in one stop, and to enhance customer service experience.

During non-peak periods, insurance core business, financial, and process management modules can be leased to other insurance companies developed in the cloud to create new profit growth points.

Under the cloud computing assistance model, the information department will no longer emerge only as a support or a behind-the-scene department. Instead, it may become a new profit center for insurance companies.

2.Cloud computing technology will create new opportunities for the development of small and medium insurance companies

With IaaS services, small and medium-sized insurance companies can rent equipment from communications providers and large insurance companies, which will save a lot of information construction costs, and more funds can be used for channel construction, product development, and customer service experience increase.

3.Cloud computing technology will support insurance companies in improving their ability to analyze big data

In the information age, the dramatically increased scale of the insurance industry's data makes insurance companies need to deal with various internal and external unstructured data and information Voice, and text and other complex images such as telephone sales and claims records, insurance contracts, claims documents, Internet sales and online customer-service records will become the main sources of data and information. The diverse, complicated and massive data and information will place higher requirements on the data processing capabilities of insurance companies.

The scalability of cloud computing enables insurance companies to collect, store, and analyze massive data and information, from which they excavate valuable information to provide sufficient storage space and computing power, further enhancing the insurance company's ability to analyze big data.

4. Cloud computing technology has made creating an "industry cloud" possible, which is conducive to promoting information sharing across the insurance industry

In the future, cloud computing technology will integrate the information sharing platforms in various provinces and realize data sharing across industries and departments, which will help to improve insurance services and the overall efficiency of the insurance industry.

The characteristics of on-demand deployment of power of cloud computing are more conducive to optimizing the allocation and utilization of resources in the insurance industry.

The sharing and openness of cloud computing keeps customers from receiving information passively. The customers needs have become the driving force behind the emergence of new financial products. Their behavior data has become the basis for insurance product and service design, and can participate in the entire process of product and service design.

The low-cost, fast, convenient, and pay-on-demand cloud computing has opened up a new channel for the "vulnerable groups" in the corporate and resident sectors to make better use of insurance products and services, enabling them to benefit from financial innovation, truly enjoy more reasonable financial services, and get their own financial rights.

7.4 Blockchain technology brings new ideas and opportunities to the development of the insurance industry

Blockchain technology is a series of data blocks generated by using cryptographic methods. Each data block contains information about a network transaction, which can verify the validity of the transaction information and generate the next block.

Blockchain technology can effectively protect the identity information of transaction participants and time-stamp and publish information on the net while recording transaction information, and it can send it to each node in the network at the same time. The nodes jointly verify to form a "consensus", thereby forming an innovative trust mechanism without the involvement of a third party.

The characteristics of blockchain technology are similar to the requirements of "mutual help insurance, data security, information transparency, reduction of management costs, and improvement of customer experience" to great extent, which are the concerns of the future development of Internet insurance.

7.4.1 Innovative application of blockchain technology in the Internet insurance industry

1. The distributed and decentralized characteristics of the blockchain make "point-to-point" transactions possible, which creates development opportunities for Internet micro mutual help insurance

"Central" institutions (or intermediaries) have specialized advantages, and it is economical for it to provide related services for the close of financial transactions. However, while "central" institutions (or intermediaries) grasp the information of each participant in the transaction, they cut off the interconnected channels between participants, hampering the flow of information and resources between participants, which is, in fact, increasing the information asymmetry in the transaction process.

The blockchain for distributed bookkeeping is a technology based on the concept of sharing. Under the constraints of established transaction rules, all transactions can be performed automatically without the need for third parties to manage or provide trust.

Transaction data is not stored on some specific servers or central nodes, but is shared among various nodes. Analyzing from this perspective, blockchain technology makes "point-to-point" transactions possible, forming "decentralized (or intermediary)" autonomous insurance organizations, providing a point-to-point risk financing solution, and creating development opportunities for micro mutual help insurance.

This type of autonomous insurance organization can allow customers with common needs and in the face of the same risks to complete insurance transactions by themselves through pre-set rules without the need for third-party intervention to achieve direct and proactive risk management.

2. Blockchain technology is conducive to strengthening the protec-

tion of customer information

Blockchain technology can ensure that the participant's information is not stolen by others. Each node in the network stores each transaction information data. However, with the setting of public and private keys, each node can only find out transaction data when querying information, and the personal information of participants is hidden which protects participants' personal information from leakage and enables participants not to be disturbed by other information when the transaction is completed.

At the level of information protection, the purchase of insurance requires the submission of real and effective identity information of the customer, as well as health status information or property information, which places higher requirements on the Internet network platform's information protection ability. Low-level information security and information leakage is a major risk currently facing the Internet insurance platform.

Blockchain technology uses a distributed intelligent identity authentication system to prevent information leakage on the basis of ensuring the authenticity of customer identity information.

The customer will verify the user name registered on the blockchain with other valid identity information, forming a "consensus" to realize the digital management of personal information. At the same time, the risk of personal information loss and tampering is also greatly reduced.

With the help of encryption technology, the customer's real identity information is hidden, and other nodes' queries are also limited to transaction information. Only the customer himself can obtain the identity information through the private key, which can effectively protect personal information.

3. Blockchain enables smart contracts to turn from virtuality to reality

A smart contract is actually a computer program that can be automatically executed when certain conditions are triggered in accordance with the established contract terms.

The emergence of smart contracts eliminates the subjective factors of personal judgment, and there will be no information forgery or tampering. Everything runs under the pre-set procedures of smart contracts, which not only makes automatic and timely settlement of claims, but also prevents fraud as well as reduces claims processing costs and makes both customers and insurance platforms more satisfied.

4. The trust mechanism built by blockchain technology can further enhance the consumer experience

Blockchain technology has created a new way of interaction between the Internet insurance platform and customers, providing customers with a new purchase experience.

After the customer purchases insurance services, all nodes in the network keep copies of the purchase behaviors which will be jointly verified and a consensus will be reached throughout the network to ensure that the purchase behavior is true and effective.

5. Blockchain technology can reduce the risk of information asymmetry on the Internet insurance platform to a certain extent

Blockchain is a public bookkeeping technology. While recording transactions, it publishes transaction information to all nodes in the network to ensure that each node can synchronize transaction information. Blockchain technology can realize the trust mechanism jointly verified by Internet insurance platforms, customers, medical examination institutions, hospitals and other related transaction parties, forming a complete insurance ecosystem.

Blockchain technology can jointly verify all transaction information with relevant transaction parties to ensure that the information is true and effective, thereby reducing the risk of information asymmetry.

6. Blockchain technology can further reduce the insurance cost of Internet

Blockchain technology can ensure that all transactions are performed in accordance with established rules, which is of great benefit to assessing customized risk and shortening the underwriting cycle. At the same time, the open and transparent rules enable blockchain to be checked by users.

Based on insurance services of blockchain, insurance policies, underwriting, and claims can basically be performed without human intervention, which can effectively avoid dishonesty and other dishonest acts, reduce insurance costs and risks faced by Internet insurance platforms, and further free up premium space.

7. Blockchain technology can ensure the security, authenticity and reliability of transaction information, and make insurance policies that can be more queried

Each node on the blockchain can verify the integrity and authenticity of the ledger to ensure that all transaction information is not tampered with, and is valid. Each node on the blockchain holds a copy of all transaction information. When the data on the blockchain and the number of participants are very large, the cost of modifying the information will be very high. At least 51% of the computing power must be mastered before the information can be modified. The cost of modification may far exceed the expected benefits. When the information is maliciously tampered with in some nudes, other nodes on the blockchain will find the information that has not formed a "consensus" and maintain and update it within a short time. Therefore, the transaction information on the blockchain is theoretically immutable.

7.4.2 Several problems that need to be solved in the promotion and application of blockchain technology in the Internet insurance industry

1. Blockchain technology has limited computing power

Analyzing the blockchain technology itself, it is difficult for the blockchain to have enough computing power to ensure the stability of the system; with less initial nodes, the risk of the blockchain being attacked and information being tampered with cannot be ignored.

Analyzing the development stage, the blockchain is still a brand-new technology, which has not yet reached the requirements of large-scale applications, and its computing capacity needs to be further improved.

2. Analyzing current developments, the role of the "central" agency of the Internet insurance platform is indispensable

The decentralization of blockchain technology removes the information asymmetry and information security risks brought by "central" institutions (or intermediaries) and improves the efficiency of financial transactions. However, it is undeniable that in the Internet insurance industry, due to mutual-help insurance still in its infancy and the impact of the "Law of Large Numbers", only insurance platforms are able to gather a large number of sample groups that face the same risks or have the same insurance needs and only they have the ability to pay claims when a large number of insurances are issued.

3. Technical risks cannot be completely avoided

Blockchain transaction rules and smart contracts are actually controlled by computer programs and languages and are automated.

Under the role of decentralization, for lack of strong guidance and control, the risk of technical and operational errors cannot be completely avoided. When the errors are not found in time, the system will continue to execute them based on the wrong procedure. The system may magnify the impact of a single input, and the cost of correcting the losses brought by these errors will be greater.

4.Subjective moral hazard still exists

Nodes on the blockchain and technical designers still have a principal-agent relationship. In the absence of effective incentives, it will be difficult for technical designers to effectively avoid loopholes in setting transaction rules.

5.Lack of blockchain laws and regulations

When the regulation lags behind the development of technology, once the blockchain is attacked and the personal information of customers is leaked, the development prospect of blockchain technology will be questioned, and the entire blockchain technology ecological environment will be greatly negatively affected.

7.5 internet of things technology will disrupt the traditional business model of the insurance industry

As an emerging science and technology that changes the mode of life, production, commerce, and economic development, the internet of things has transformed from "interconnection of people" to "interconnection of things", which is of great significance across the times.

In the future, the internet of things will become one of the main driving forces for innovation and change in the world. With the widespread application of smart devices in homes, businesses, cities, and countries, it is bound to affect the traditional business model of the insurance industry.

7.5.1 What is IoT technology?

1.Concept

The internet of things technology is the Internet technology that make things connected to each other, that is, based on the Internet the user end is extended to between items, so that the information can be exchanged.

2.Multi-level analysis of the internet of things

(1)Technical level: The internet of things uses radio frequency identification, infrared sensor, global positioning system, laser scanner, gas sensor and other information sensing equipment to connect items with the internet of things according to the agreed protocol for information exchange and communication, so as to realize intelligent identification, positioning, tracking, monitoring and management.

(2)Connection object level: The internet of things can connect between items, between people and objects, and between people.

(3)Application level: The internet of things technology will make full use of a series of emerging Internet technologies in the fields of transportation, environmental protection, public safety, fire protection, smart home and water and power supply , embed intelligent information sensing equipment in articles, and then use Internet technology realize "interconnection of things" and "interconnection between people and things". In the internet of things system, the data information of people and things is collected and analyzed in real time through big data technology, so that people and things can be "intelligently managed" in a more refined and dynamic way to improve the efficiency of resource utilization.

3.Analyze the disruptive impact of IoT technology on the insurance industry from the concept and characteristics of IoT technology

(1)The IoT technology can reduce the information asymmetry between insurance companies and customers, increase the number of exchanges, and transform the "weak connection" relationship between the insurance industry and customers into a "strong connection" relationship.

(2) The internet of things technology can reduce customers risks and help achieve risk reduction management.

(3)The internet of things technology helps to optimize the business processes of the insurance industry, improve the risk management level of insurance companies, continuously improve the customer experience, and enhance the overall competitiveness of insurance companies.

7.5.2 Wearable device upends the business model of health insurance

Concept: daily wearable devices that use wearable technology to intelligently design people's daily wear and collect human biological signals.

common forms are smart bracelets, watches, glasses, gloves, shoes and clothing. Some wearable devices exist alone, like mobile phones and pedometers.

The emergence and development of wearable devices will become an important driving force for innovation in China's health insurance market:

1.Development of wearable devices will innovate health management model

Realize "smart medicine"(portable dynamic electrocardiogram, implantable blood glucose monitor)

Performance: With the development and popularization of wearable devices, based on Internet, internet of things and modern medical technology, by integrating wearable devices, call centers, emergency centers, and medical institutions, a set of remote health assistance service system integrating prevention, monitoring, diagnosis, rescue, and rehabilitation guidance can be established to help patients monitor their own health without leaving home, reducing the number of hospital visits; by uploading health data to the cloud, an electronic health file is formed, and with the help of remote interactive technology, you can directly talk to the doctor at home, making online doctor-seeing possible.

2. The popularity of wearable devices will be an important way to get data for the insurance industry

Insurance companies obtain valuable information through data processing, analysis, integration, mining and other technologies and discover customers' insurance needs, providing customers with personalized and customized health insurance service solutions and big data foundations.

In the field of health insurance, wearable devices will become an important "entrance" for data collection. According to the program, wearable devices can automatically collect the corresponding health data of customers, not only forming structured data that can be expressed by numbers and symbols, but also forming graphics, charts, voice, film and video and other diversified non-structured data.

3. Application of wearable devices will make differentiated pricing of health insurance possible

Wearable devices can collect customer health, diet, exercise status and other information in real time and upload it to the cloud, realizing "digitalization" of customer health status, accurately assessing customer health risk status, and using risk status as the basis of insurance products pricing that helps break the traditional pricing model of health insurance products.

Under the differentiated pricing model based on wearable devices, the insurance rate applicable to high-risk customers is higher than that of low-risk ones, and the insurance services enjoyed by the two types of customers are the same, which is helpful to attract more customers facing the same risks. As the number of customers increases, the average insurance rate will inevitably continue to decline, health insurance products and service innovations will continue to emerge, and the customer group will collectively benefit, thereby forming a virtuous circle of health insurance development.

4. Wearable devices will help the insurance industry achieve precision marketing

With the deep application of big data technology in the insurance industry, data collected by wearable devices will become an important basis for insurance companies to formulate precise marketing strategies.

The data collected by the insurance company through the wearable device, such as health, environmental and exercise status, connected with the personal information provided by customers when they register for the wearable device, the insurance company can predict the customer's insurance needs, and discover the "pain points" of the customer, and recommend the right health insurance products to customers at a right time.

5. Wearable devices will provide a basis for risk reduction management methods

Wearable devices have fostered a healthy lifestyle of customers to a certain extent, fundamentally reducing customer risk levels.

Wearable devices that include positioning functions will automatically remind customers of potential risks in their area, promptly issue early warning information, implement pre-crisis management, avoid potential risks into accidents, and effectively achieve risk reduction management.

6. Wearable devices will help improve the customer experience

The remote health management platforms integrating wearable devices, call centers, emergency centers, and medical institutions, which can directly read the personal electronic health records of customers, and provide one-stop medical and health management services.

Through the real-time updated electronic health file, once abnormal indicators are found, the relevant information will be directly transferred to the online expert database. The experts will directly connect with customers through video, audio and other methods for "one-to-one" diagnosis and follow-up treatment, saving customers the cost of medical treatment.

Insurance companies can promptly promote personalized and customized health insurance products to customers based on their health data collected by wearable devices, effectively enhancing the customer purchase experience.

Risk reduction management function of wearable devices can inspire customers to form healthy habits, achieve health goals, improve their health, and realize true "health management".

7.5.3 Development and application of connected cars in the insurance industry

The Internet of Vehicles is the application of the internet of things in the automotive industry. The Internet of Vehicles is a huge interactive network composed of information such as vehicle position, speed, and route, and can achieve wireless communication and information exchange between vehicles, between roads and vehicles, and between people and vehicles.

The application of the Internet of Vehicles not only changes the traditional automobile industry, but also profoundly affects the insurance industry. It will change the pricing model of automobile insurance, promote the improvement of risk management and insurance services, help social management, and comprehensively promote the upgrading of the insurance industry.

1. The application of connected cars will promote the reform of auto insurance pricing model

(1) The pricing of auto insurance is affected by the specifications of the motor vehicle. The use and size of the vehicle will directly determine the "compulsory motor vehicle liability insurance". Motor vehicle insurance premiums are also affected by car owners.

(2) Under the traditional pricing model, the actual driving conditions of the vehicle such as the annual driving mileage, the number of rapid acceleration / emergency braking within 100 kilometers, the driving speed, and the frequently traveled roads have not become the factors that determine the pricing of auto insurance. It is obviously unfair to apply the same rate to motor vehicles with the same vehicle type and usage but different risk conditions. To some extent, low-risk customers have actually assumed part of the premiums for high-risk customers.

(3) The transformation of the pricing model promoted by the Internet of Vehicles includes changes in the data foundation, innovation in pricing basis, and improvement in pricing frequency. Based on the Internet of Vehicles technology, auto insurance products will no longer rely on only a few data to price, but will use big data analysis technology for accurate pricing based on multi-dimensional, high-precision mass data; auto insurance products will no longer rely solely on historical data to price. Instead, it is based on real-time updated data; the pricing frequency of auto insurance products will change the past calculation model based on years, and achieve a slightly weathered pricing model

based on daily or even single trips.

(4) Insurance Company analyzes the above data, comprehensively evaluates the potential driving risk of the driver, and combines traditional factors such as vehicle models and accident records to formulate different insurance rates through models to make auto insurance pricing more scientific and fair, providing customers with more options, so that low-risk customers may get cheaper rates and enhance the competitiveness of auto insurance products.

2.The application of connected cars will help insurance companies achieve risk reduction management

(1) OBD equipment can collect real-time data on vehicle conditions, driving sections, driving mileage, rapid acceleration / sudden braking times within 100 kilometers, and the driving speed. Big data analysis technology can enable insurance companies to master the driving habits of drivers. Through real-time monitoring, alarm alerts, and other functions, once the customer launches a dangerous driving behavior, it can immediately call the police, thereby intervening in and correcting the dangerous driving behaviors, and can positively guide the customer to drive safely through the rate lever, which essentially reduces the customer's risk level.

(2) The Internet of Vehicles can also predict the risks by detecting vehicle safety conditions and issuing disaster warnings to avoid accidents occurrence and achieve risk reduction management.

3.Application of connected car technology will improve the overall risk management level of the insurance industry

(1) The Internet of Vehicles technology will comprehensively improve the risk management level of insurance companies.

(2) In terms of underwriting and pricing, with the help of connected car technology, risk identification and assessment can be performed

more effectively, thereby enhancing the risk selection capabilities of insurance companies.

(3)In the process of disaster and loss prevention, the connected car technology is used to participate in customer risk management and make effective pre-disaster prevention, which can reduce risk accidents. In the process of the rescue and claims, through the real-time monitoring and positioning of the Internet of Vehicles, the vehicle's position information can be obtained at the first time of an accident, and rescue work can be started to minimize the accident losses.

4.Connected car technology helps reduce the risk of insurance fraud

(1)The main cause of insurance fraud is that insurance companies do not have comprehensive information on insured accidents, giving the insured the opportunity to exaggerate insurance losses or even intentionally create insured accidents. Therefore, comprehensive and truthful data acquisition is the key to tackling insurance fraud.

(2)The application of the Internet of Vehicles technology can fundamentally improve the information asymmetry between the insurance company and the policyholder, and improve the information disadvantaged position of the insurance company. The trajectory playback and data analysis before the accident can reconstruct and restore the information of the insurance accident scene and enhance the insurance company's ability to identify insurance fraud.

5.Connected car technology will help insurance companies innovate service content

(1)The application of Internet of Vehicles will increase the contact points between insurance companies and customers, and enrich the content of insurance services. Under the traditional auto insurance model, there is a "weak connection" between the insurance company and the customer. Only when the car insurance product is purchased and an accident claim occurs, the "connection" occurs, and the customer has the opportunity to enjoy the services provided by the insurance company. Generally speaking, high-quality customers who do not have accidents or have fewer accidents, however, enjoy less services than customers who frequently make insurance claims. By providing connected cars and follow-up services, insurance companies will increase contact with customers and frequency, forming a "strong connection" between them, understand customer needs in depth, and provide personalized value-added services to customers, and enhance the customer experience, and then improve its ability to serve customers.

(2)The Internet of Vehicles can effectively integrate offline insurance service resources and expand insurance service. Insurance companies have a wealth of customer information such as vehicle underwriting claims, and vehicle loss as well as data and service resources such as car repair and rescue services. Through the connected cars, insurance companies can build a connected car service system centered on car insurance and based on the car insurance ecological environment, make full use of the third-party supplier system, integrate service resources, and provide customers with value-added services based on car-based life cycles and related industries, extend the service functions of insurance, and further enhance the competitiveness of insurance companies.

The Fourth Part
Cases

Chapter 8 Cases of Financial Technology

8.1 Typical examples of financial technology abroad

At present, major representative Fintech companies abroad mainly include Wealthfront, the originator of intelligent financial management, ABRA, cross-border payment under the blockchain, Mint, artificial intelligence application, and Lending Club, an Internet loan company.

8.1.1 Wealthfront, the originator of smart investment advisers

Robo-advice2090：20902008200520082015 Wealthfront Betterment Future Advisor Blackrock Future Advisor 2015

Robo-advice can also be called robotic advisory, intelligent financial management or automatic wealth management. By big data analysis, quantitative financial models, and intelligent algorithms, a series of intelligent algorithms, portfolio optimization and other theoretical models are used, according to investors' risk tolerance levels, expected return targets, and investment style preferences, to provide users with investment references and monitor market dynamics, automatically re-balance asset allocation, and improve return rate on assets, allowing investors to achieve "zero-based, zero-cost, expert-level" dynamic asset investment allocation. The process for platform users to make investments is roughly the same, which can be divided into six major steps: risk assessment, investment plans obtainment, accounts connection, investing, plans update, and investments completion. Since the late 1990s,

Robo-Advice has gone through three stages: The first is online robotic advice stage (from late 1990s to 2008), when the technical level and scale of online investment analysis tools have begun to expand. Some companies began to provide online robotic advice services. In 2005 when allowing securities traders to directly give investment analysis tools for investors, the scale of online asset management services expanded rapidly. The second is robotic investment advisory stage (from 2008 to 2015), when The "robotic investment advisory" company represented by Wealthfront and Betterment Future Advisor began to develop, providing customers with various machine learning-based robotic investment advisory tools directly. Some traditional securities dealers themselves developed the tools or entered the field through M&A, such as Intelligent Portfolio Services introduced by Charles Schwab and Future Advisor acquired by Blackrock; The third is Robo-Advice stage(since 2015), when big data-based deep learning is relied on and computing power brought by cloud computing has greatly improved, making artificial intelligence achieve breakthrough again. At present, more and more companies are beginning to try to develop artificial intelligence investment systems that can completely separate from human in the investment management chain. Artificial intelligence such as Wealthfront is pushing automatic financial management into the third stage to development.

1.A brief introduction to Wealthfront

Wealthfront Spark Capital Kaching 2011 Wealthfront Andy Rachleff Benchmark Capital Burton Malkiel Wealthfront Palo.

Wealthfront is mainly invested by Spark Capital, which was formerly Kaching Investment Consulting Company. In 2011, Wealthfront transformed into a prqfessional online wealth management company, one of the earliest Robo-advice platforms in the United States. Wealthfront founder Andy Rachleff was one of the founders of Benchmark

Capital and a teacher at Stanford Business School. The company's management team consists of industry and academic celebrities such as Chief Investment Officer Burton Malkiel writing "Walking Wall Street". Wealthfront is located in Palo Alto, California, mainly targeted middle-income young people, not high-net-worth individuals. Wealthfront has developed rapidly and achieved very good results. As of January 2015, Wealthfront's assets were only \$ 1.83 billion; as of the end of February 2016, however, the asset was close to \$ 3 billion

2.Main business of Wealthfront

Wealthfront uses modern portfolio theory (MPT) to recommend investment portfolios to users. Through diversified portfolios, it reduces risks without reducing expected returns. Investors can achieve higher returns at the same level of risk, or carry a lower risk at the same level of returns. Wealthfront chooses up to 11 types of assets, which, on the one hand, helps to increase the degree of diversification and reduce risks, and on the other hand, provides users with more asset portfolio options to meet the more needs of risk preference type users .

The main products and services provided by Wealthfront are automatic portfolio financial management advisory services, including opening, managing accounts and evaluating portfolios for users. Users can invest through the Wealthfront platform with the subject ETF fund. In addition, it provides services including tax loss harvesting, direct indexing of tax optimization, and single stock diversification investment. The carrier of Wealthfront's investment portfolio is various index fund ETFs, covering asset classes from U.S. , overseas, emerging market stocks, U.S. Treasuries and emerging market bonds to U.S. inflation indexed bonds, natural resources, real estate, corporate bonds and municipal Bonds. In addition, wealthfront has provided other services.

The company's platform charges customers consulting fees in proportion to the net asset value: when the assets are less than $10,000, the platform does not charge consulting fees; when the assets are more than $10,000, the platform collects 0.25% of the annual consulting fee; For promotion, Wealthfront also introduced a preferential policy, that is, for every user invited, the inviter will get reduced by $5,000 of a consulting fee for the investment.

8.1.2 Cross-border payment based on blockchain technology ABRA

Blockchain is the basic technology of digital currency Bitcoin, which is essentially a decentralized database. Through blockchain technology, cross-border payment, settlement and clearing can be directly made between the two account banks, bypassing intermediary, clearing, settlement banks and SWIFT, reducing handling fees in the process of transfer and realizing round-the-clock payment, real-time account arrival, easy withdrawal, and no hidden costs, which is also helpful to reduce cross-border e-commerce fund risk and meet convenience needs.

1.A profile of ABRA

Founded in 2014, ABRA was mainly invested from Tata, American Express, First Round Capital, and Jungle Ventures. Through blockchain technology and shared ATM networks, ABRA allows users to deposit and withdraw money anytime and anywhere, or make cross-border remittances in a more convenient way. At present, ABRA has been materialized in the Philippines and the United States.

2.Main business of ABRA

Users use the ABRA App to store currency in digital form on their mobile phones to remit money to any ABRA account bundled with a mobile phone number around the world via the Abra Teller network (a shared ATM network established by ABRA) or traditional bank routing, or convert the digital currency into cash. During the payment, remittance or withdrawal period, the app will instantly generate a blockchain-based smart contract, and the assigned counterparty will ensure that the value of the user's funds will not be changed by the bitcoin price within three days by means of hedging. For example, Teller cash withdrawal, users find the nearby ABRA Teller through the ARA application and face-to-face transfers money in exchange for bitcoin. If you need to withdraw money, you can also find ABRA Tell in the same way to exchange bitcoin for cash. ABRA Teller can charge users a certain percentage of fees.

8.1.3 Artificial intelligence applications – Mint

Artificial intelligence is a technical science that researches and develops theories, methods, technologies, and application systems for simulating, extending, and expanding human intelligence, which is a branch of computer science. Artificial intelligence attempts to hit the essence of intelligence and produce a new type of intelligent machine that can respond to human intelligence in a similar way, with robotics, voice recognition, image recognition, natural language processing, and expert systems as the targeted research field.

1.A profile of Mint

Mint founder Hardeep Walia was a former Microsoft executive who was in charge of investment and M&A related to corporate development strategy. Another co-founder Tariq Hilaly was the Vice President of Alliance Bernstein hedge fund. Mint is also a portfolio service provider, whose portfolio is called Motif, focusing on establishing a social stock selection investment platform. Since its official launch in the United States in June 2012, users have created countless Motif (investment portfolios). A Motif contains multiple securities (including stocks, and securities, up to 30) with similar themes or concepts, such as cloud computing, mobile Internet and 3D printing.

2.Main business of Mint

Users can choose existing Motif from Mint platform and use it directly according to their investment philosophy, or modify (including adjusting the stock / fund composition and proportion contained in it) and use it, and they can create their own new Motif. The novelty of this platform lies in: First, it provides a powerful self-service portfolio design tool, which is convenient for users to easily, intuitively modify, create, and evaluate Motif, which only takes a few minutes to have a personalized portfolio; the second is the introduction of a social mechanism. Users can share their Motif to friends or selected circles, and everyone discusses and improves Motif together. In essence, Mint is the application of advanced technology and social mechanisms to help each user become their own fund manager. Its charging strategy is also very unique. Regardless of the total investment amount of a user in a Motif (a minimum investment amount of not less than $250), and whether the Motif is provided by the platform or customized by the user, the platform will charge $0.95 each time a user buys or sells according to the Motif For stock / fund portfolios. If you only trade one of these securities, you will be charged $ 4.95 each time.

8.1.4 P2P Online lending platform – Lending Club

P2P online lending is that users can complete the various steps of a loan application without the need for going out based on the advantages of the Internet, including understanding the application conditions for various types of loans, preparing application materials, and submitting loan applications, which can be completed efficiently on the Internet.

1.A profile of Lending Club

Lending Club was founded by Laplanche in 2006 and is a San Francisco-based Fintech company, which included Internet queen Mary Meeker, former Morgan Stanley CEO John Mack, and former US Secretary of the Treasury Larry Summers as the members of boards. Lending Club was listed on the New York Stock Exchange in 2014, the first listed P2P online lending platform. At the initial stage, Lending Club only offered personal loans of two, three, and five years which were mostly used for refinancing and repaying credit cards with a loan amount ranging from ＄1,000 to ＄35,000. Since the beginning of 2014, Lending Club has officially entered the corporate loan service.

2.Main business of Lending Club

Lending Club is essentially an Internet platform for everyone applying for loans. Its main business model is the platform model. By matching borrowers and investors to obtain intermediary fees, it has established a set of financing platforms outside the banking system.

Lending Club checks credit and determines the interest rate when the borrower makes an application, but it will find a bank to issue the loan, and then buy the debt from the bank to make itself a creditor. There is actually no credit risk for the bank. And this is done after the investor pays. For the Lending Club Fintech case, there is no credit risk, and the risk rests entirely with investors. For all loans, the borrower borrows money from LendingClub, in which investors also invest, so even if the borrower repays the money, if the Lending Club has some financial problems, the investor may be at risk. Most of Lending Club's loans are funded by institutional investors, which may be pension companies, asset management companies, or hedge funds. Lending Club itself does not bear any risk of default, it just makes money through trading commissions, and makes from both. For investors,

Lending Club charges a 1% service fee. For lenders, Lending Club will charge a product setup fee when the loan is issued, usually 1% to 5%.

8.1.5 fintech companies

Technology companies that challenge banking have not yet appeared in the United States, mainly related to regulation, and many have assembled in Europe.

The first is fidor bank. Digital banks started operating in Germany in 2009, mainly focusing on opening customers, actively participating in bank decision-making and rebuilding customer confidence in banking. Currently their product portfolio includes commercial and personal ones, and customers' banking business covers cheques and savings account loans and bonds, which has more than 100,000 customers and 300,000 members. Fidor has a bank license similar to traditional banks. Unlike traditional banks, to encourage customers to sign up and make the user members active, they provide 50 euros to help shoot users-themed films. When Facebook is clicked 2000 times, the bank raises the savings rate and lowers the loan rate.

The second is RoCKet bank, an online bank from Russia. Due to their customer service style and viral marketing, it is called a chic bank.

The third is atom bank founded in Durham, UK, one of the exclusive banks, with consumers aged between 18 and 24 as the main users. It provides financial products, which can be bought by users through APP, which mainly include fixed savings accounts and mortgages.

In terms of payment and remittance, the main Fintech companies are as follows.

The first is transfer wise which was founded in January 2011. It is a P2P Fintech company, whose remittance exchange is headquartered in London. It currently has offices in Sydney, Estonia, Singapore and New

York with at least 1 million customers per month and transfers of 800 million pounds, supporting 47 currencies.

The second is PayPal at the forefront of an international money transfer, which follows a policy to acquire the best company they can find, providing power and collaboration to its business model.

The third is ripple. Founded in 2012, it is a US-based company that provides network protocols to connect different financial systems and secure fund transfers in different countries .

The other is some social media-based remittances such as the big whatsAPP, Facebook, We Chat and viber.

8.2 Typical Fintech cases domestically

8.2.1 Ant Financial

Its the parent company of Ant financial services group. A typical case study is Zhejiang Alibaba E-Commerce Co., Ltd., whose predecessor was Xiaowei Finance, which started from Alipay. In October 2014, Ant Financial was formally established with the vision of "bringing small and beautiful changes to the world" and was committed to creating an open ecosystem. At the beginning of the establishment of Ant Financial, it was only the settlement department of Taobao. It had only a few employees and used a simple electronic form for bookkeeping. But in just ten years, it started in the payment field and entered the financial industry and changed the face of China's financial industry via data and technology, especially by mobile internet, big data, and cloud computing. Since its establishment, Ant Financial's products and services have become an important practice in Fintech.

8.2.1.1 Main business of Ant Financial

Ant Financial is transformed by users of e-commerce platforms, accumulating a large amount of personal and online payment transaction data, using big data to derive value, and carrying out a variety of Internet financial services, including Alipay, a life service platform, Ant Jubao, a smart wealth management platform, Ant Financial Cloud, a cloud computing service platform, Sesame Credit, an independent third-party credit evaluation system, and MYbank. In addition, Ant Financial also works with investing and affiliated companies to cooperate at the business and service levels to deeply integrate and promote the prosperity of the business ecosystem. As the earliest Internet financial platform in China, Ant Financial has already owned Alipay, Yu'ebao, Zhaocaibao, Ant Fortune, MYbank, Ant Credit Pay, Sesame Credit, Ant Financial Cloud, Antsdaq, and many other business sectors, covering almost all sectors of the traditional financial industry, and has become the first unicorn among domestic Fintech companies.

1.Alipay

Alipay relies on the Internet to initiate payment instructions to realize the transfer of monetary funds between consumers and merchants. It is mainly divided into the following steps: (1) the buyer browses the product on the webpage and selects the required product, fills the order and pays to Alipay; (2) Alipay notifies the seller of the shipment, and the seller delivers the goods according to the order requirements, waiting for the buyer to confirm the receipt; (3) If the buyer is satisfied with the product and confirms the receipt in Alipay, the payment will be made to the seller by Alipay. The transaction ends; (4) If the buyer applies for return after checking the product, after the buyer and seller negotiate, the seller agrees to return the goods. Then Alipay refunds the purchase price to the buyer.

2. Yu'E Bao

Yu'ebao is a balance value-added service created by Alipay. Transferring the money into Yu'ebao means buying the Yu'ebao currency fund provided by Tianhong Fund and earning income. The funds in Yu'ebao can also be used for online shopping payment at any time, and can be withdrawn flexibly.

3. Zhao Cai Bao

Zhao Cai Bao is an open financial information service platform that can provide users with flexible and regular financial information services. There are two main types of investment on the Zhaocaibao platform. The first category is loan products issued by SMEs and individuals through this platform. Financial institutions and guarantee companies are the credit enhancement institutions to provide principal and interest payment and credit enhancement measures; The second one is wealth management products released by various financial institutions or those which have been recognized by financial regulators through this platform. Investors can choose to lend funds directly to financiers or purchase wealth management products through this platform according to their preference for risks.

4. Ant fortune

Ant Fortune is a one-stop mobile wealth management platform that integrates Yu'ebao, Zhaocaibao, funds, and stocks, which correspond to different levels of financial needs such as current, regular, funds, and stocks respectively, officially launched on August 18, 2015.

5. MYbank

MYbank officially opened on June 25, 2015, which is one of the first five private piloted banks in China. It adopts a "small deposit and small loan" business model, with small and micro enterprises and individuals on e-commerce as consumers and customers, providing personal deposit products below 200,000 yuan and loan products below 5 million yuan.

6.Ant Credit Pay

Ant Credit Pay is an online shopping service provided by Ant Small Loan to consumers to "buy this month and pay it back next month"(pay next month upon confirming receipt). Ant Small Loan undertakes the mission of Alibaba Group to provide Internet-based, batch-oriented, and digital financial services for small and micro enterprises and online individual entrepreneurs. Since its development, Ant Small Loan has successively developed small loan products such as Ali Credit Loan, MYbank Loan, Taobao (Tmall) Credit Loan and Taobao (Tmall) Order Loan.

7.Sesame Credit

Sesame Credit is a society-oriented credit service system. Based on information from different sources, it uses big data and cloud computing technology to objectively present the individual's credit status. By connecting various services, everyone is allowed to experience the value brought by credit. Sesame Credit Score (in short: Sesame Score) is the credit score obtained by the company after processing, sorting, and calculating the personal user information currently collected, ranging from 350 to 950 points. The higher score represents the better credit level. The higher Sesame score can help individuals get more efficient and better services.

8.Ant Financial Cloud

Ant Financial Cloud covers the entire set of technical services required for the development, operation, and management of financial business systems, which can greatly reduce the difficulty of R&D and management of financial systems in a distributed environment. At the same time, the security, consistency, continuity, reliability and other characteristics of financial system-level standards, as well as the highly concurrent, online, real-time interaction capabilities required by the mobile era, are integrated into the technology platform, which it also covers. "Shanghai Cloud" financial institutions only need to pay far less than the cost of traditional financial technology, so that they can have the ability to process high concurrent financial transactions and massive large data, which greatly enhances financial business innovation and risk control capabilities.

9.Antsdaq

Antsdaq uses equity as a connection tool to help companies find upward funding sources, open up the upstream and downstream resources of the industry chain, connect the core high-value users of the enterprise, and help enterprises to solve various problems in the growth cycle. Specifically speaking, enterprises can raise funds through Antsdaq, and get full support from production, channels, operations, brands and other links; investors can find investment opportunities through Antsdaq, understand enterprises that they recognized and invested based on their understanding of specific industries and share their growth.

8.2.1.2 News from Ant Financial

On May 19, 2015, Ant Financial announced that it will launch Antsdaq, an online equity crowdfunding platform, which will cooperate with IDG, Sequoia and other start-up investment institutions and Taobao crowdfunding, Maker + and other platforms to provide financing services for start-up projects from the start-up financing to product sales throughout the growth cycle. On November 18, 2015, the internet equity financing platform Antsdaq went online for testing. In 2015, Ant Financial announced the launch of the "Internet Thruster" program, which will strengthen cooperation with financial institutions at the channel, technology, data, credit, and even capital level to help financial institutions and partners accelerate their "Internet +" plans. In five years, it will help more than 1,000 financial institutions to provide inclusive financial services for small and micro enterprises and individual consumers. In 2016, Ant Financial launched the "Spring Rain Plan", which plans to invest 1 billion yuan in cash to support ecological partners, helps at least 1 million developers in 3 years, and serves 10 million small and medium businesses and institutions. On July 8, 2016, Ant Financial and Jiashi Fund jointly announced that they will further deepen their strategic cooperation. Ant Financial has invested in the "Gold Beta" of Jiashi Fund to become the only new shareholder in the first round of financing of Golden Beta. According to people with knowledge of the matter, Ant Financial's total investment amount is 100 million yuan, accounting for 20% of the shares; in 2017, Christine Lagarde, president of the International Monetary Fund (IMF), announced the establishment of a group of senior advisers to lead financial technology, and Ant Financial is the only member from China.

8.2.2 Lakala

Lakala is an leading comprehensive Internet financial service platform in the industry, which was one of the first companies to obtain a third-party payment license issued by the central bank. It has long been ranked among the top three in the domestic third-party mobile payment field and the acquisition industry transaction scale. Lakala was founded in 2005. The earliest origin was to use a handheld mobile terminal to pay back credit cards, instead of paying at bank counters, making it convenient to repay credit cards. After that, it was extended to pay back credit cards and pay utility bills at convenience stores. Later, it learned from Square in the United States as a personal handheld payment terminal. And then it applied for an acquisition license, and started to do merchant acceptance and extended to online-to-online e-commerce, such as buying train tickets in the community. At present, Lakala adheres to the concepts of inclusiveness, science, technology, innovation and integration, relies on technological innovation, and secure risk control as the guarantee. Through the multiple channels of online + offline and software + hardware development, Lakala has created a unified bottom-level, user-oriented symbiosis system that provides honest, transparent, secure, and innovative financial services to individual and corporate users.

8.2.2.1 Main business of Lakala

As a comprehensive financial service platform, Lakala focuses on financial innovation, promotes the development of the Internet + Finance model with three innovations such as financial technology, product-side, and service innovation, and is involved in equity crowdfunding, supply chain finance, and financing leasing, asset exchange and other fields, covering many fields such as payment, wealth management, credit reporting, financing, and community finance.

Backed by huge platform transaction data and the continuous development of credit reporting business, Lakala has built a comprehensive credit evaluation model, which has greatly enhanced the platform's risk control level. While providing comprehensive financial services to individual users and small and micro enterprises, Lakala combines the large amount of large data accumulated over many years with a credit reporting model and incorporates user credit information and business logic and other assessment standards to form unique "big data + credit reporting risk control system" to ensure the rapid development of related services across the platform. Lakala Fintech not only uses massive data as a risk control support, but also models based on it to make the model dynamic and actively prevent and control front fraud risk and back credit risk.

As a carrier of Internet financial services, Lakala has built and continues to innovate a multi-credit consumption system that is contextualized. In order to meet the diversified credit needs of users, Lakala focuses on financial needs and actively explores credit products in different payment scenarios, introducing differentiated credit products such as "repay for you, easy installment, pay for you, employee loans and student loans", and covering users with strong demand for medium and long-term and large loans.as far as possible, to

It can be seen from Lakala's fastest-growing credit business that platform products can meet the diverse financing needs of users. From short-term reimbursement services based on weeks to large loan services with annual settlement cycles, users can be provided with 1,000 to 300,000 yuan loan service. Take the "repay for you" business for example. Based on the analysis of the user's repayment amount and repayment period, the product design tends to be small, fast, and flexible, which effectively solves problems such as credit card repayment difficulties.

8.2.2.2 News of Lakala

The rapid development of Lakala's financial business benefits from its risk control management system accumulated over the years and its efficient, large-capacity credit system that can support large numbers of customers and calculations, forming business barriers that have the industry advantages of the financial through differentiated risk pricing and achieving deep integration with the financial industry through scientific and technological means. In March 2015, Lakala announced that it would seek to transform from a third-party payment company to a comprehensive Internet + financial group, with electronic payment, Internet finance and community e-commerce O2O as its new business lines. In April of the same year, Lakala launched a P2P online lending platform to focus on personal small loan business, and its Koala Credit Card, along with Alibaba's Sesame Credit, won the Central Bank's first batch of personal credit permission licenses. In 2016, with the accumulated massive financial data, through the refined risk measurement tools and decision analysis technology, Lakala launched the second-generation risk control system "Eagle Eye" risk control system, which is based on the first-generation risk control system. Lakala uses the "4V" feature of big data to achieve efficient and low-cost risk prevention to promote Lakala's business to transform from being driven from a multidimensional scoring model to an optimization drive, and from a single point of decision-making to the upgrade of enterprise-level decision-making, which has further enhanced the platform's risk control security level and laid the foundation for the rapid and stable development of the platform.

8.2.3 Jingdong(JD) Finance

JD Finance is a subsidiary of the JD Group. Through emerging technologies such as the application of big data, machine learning, artificial intelligence, and blockchain, it has established a set of financial infrastructure such as a unique big data system, technology mechanism, risk control system, payment system, and investment research system, providing banks, securities, insurance and other financial institutions and other non-financial institutions with technologies, products, users, funds, and assets and menu-based, embedded services. JD Finance is a subsidiary of the JD Group, which started operating independently in October 2013 with factoring, small loan, payment, and corporate credit licenses. It also has a number of subsidiaries including insurance financing companies and small loan companies. JD Finance belongs to a Fintech company, relying on the JD ecological platform. Based on data and technology, it builds an open ecosystem that serves financial institutions and non-financial institutions.

8.2.3.1 Main business of JD Finance

JD Finance has established supply chain finance, consumer finance, crowdfunding, wealth management, payment, insurance, securities and other business sectors. It successively launched Jingbaobei, Baitiao, JD Wallet, Small Treasury, Jingxiaodai, crowdfunding related to rights and interests, equity crowdfunding, crowdfunding insurance and other products, as well as JD maker ecosystem to provide customers with financing loans, crowdfunding, financial management, payment and other financial services.

1.Supply chain finance

JD supply chain finance mainly includes "Jingbaobei", "Jingxiaodai", and chattel financing, of which the "Jingbaobei" launched at the end of 2013 mainly includes multiple products such as receivable accounts pool financing, order pool financing, single financing, and sales financing; the "Jingxiaodai" launched in 2014 provided e-commerce platform sellers with small loan; In September 2015, JD Finance and China Post Express Logistics jointly created the first big data-based e-commerce company's movable property financing model.

2.Consumer Finance

JD Finance's main product is "Jingdong baitiao", and its business is broadly divided into two categories: "Jingdong baitiao" launched in early 2014 and "baitiao +" which are successively launched. "Jingdong baitiao" belongs to the credit of receivables and is operated with Jingdong's own funds; "baitiao +" (such as campus, travel, rental, and down payment baitiao) have Jingdong's Jinghui small loan company behind, issuing loans double the leverage rate of small loan companies.

3.Crowdfunding

Jingdong Crowdfunding can provide targeted, complete and continuous financial technology service support at different stages of the company's development process, covering data support, market inspection, resource integration and other whole entrepreneurial support services. JD Finance has formed an ecological strategic layout of four major systems: product crowdfunding, JD dongjia, Zhongchuang shengtai, and Zhongchuang Funds, with equity crowdfunding, product crowdfunding, blind funding, credit crowdfunding, and unlimited funding as its main products.

4.Wealth Management

Relying on the transaction data and credit system accumulated by the JD Group on the e-commerce platform and the professional experience of the wealth management team, JD Finance provides Internet wealth management to users, including JD small treasury, fund wealth management, bill wealth management, insurance wealth management, and fixed income wealth management.

5.Payment

JD Finance has launched a cross-platform secure and convenient payment product that is compatible with PC and the mainstream environment and wireless terminals, with five characteristics of fast payment, good experience, wide dimensions, security and simplified standard access, forming several product lines such as online payment, fast payment, and mobile payment matrix.

6.Insurance

JD Finance has launched five first innovative Internet insurance productscrowdfunding bouncing canceling insurance, investment credit protection insurance, overseas shopping protection insurance, home worry-free protection insurance and 30-day products return insurance.

7.Securities

JD Finance's stock platform launched cai, which provides technical services and communication for professional securities practitioners, including private equity fund researchers and securities analysts, and provides simulated operations and investment education for ordinary users.

8.2.3.2 News of JD Finance

In January 2016, JD Finance raised 6.65 billion yuan, led by Sequoia Capital China Fund, Jiashi Investment, and China TaipingLife Insurance Co., Ltd. After the transaction, JD Group still controls most equity in JD Finance; in March 2016, JD baitiao upgrade to launch an independent domain name; in April 2016, JD Finance launched the first domestic Internet insurance financing business ABS on the Shanghai Stock Exchange; in May 2016, two securities industry products were released, which are JD Finance Big Data consumption index and quantitative strategy development platform respectively; In July 2016, JD maker platform was officially launched to provide various services needed for entrepreneurship. In November 2016, JD Finance and U.S. big data company ZestFinance jointly launched a joint venture consumer finance company ZRobot; in December 2016, it launched the high-end financial service platform Dongjia Fortune, and "Dongjia Fortune" official website; In 2017, based on financial technology and relied on JD big data and artificial intelligence technology, JD crowdfunding launched the JD Custom section to realize the effective combination of multi-party resources such as high-quality merchants, forward-looking high-quality products, financial investment, and mall channels in the JD ecosystem to maximize the consumer experience of users. In 2017, JD Finance launched the industry's first self-operating platform for financial institutions "JD expert", covering fund information, investment research strength demonstration, fund product introduction, fund manager interviews, fund product diagnosis, robo-advice, operating activities and other sectors to provide free services to financial institutions such as fund companies, insurance companies and private equity to quickly establish and operate the mobile official website.

8.2.4 Tencent

Tencent was established in November 1998. Through instant messaging tools QQ, mobile social and communication services We Chat, portal Tencent. com (QQ. com), Tencent games, social networking platform QQ space and other network platforms to meet the Internet user needs of communication, access to information, entertainment and finance.

8.2.4.1 Main business of Tencent

Tencent's financial business mainly includes We Chat payment, the payment sector with QQ wallet as the representative and Tencent Wealth Management, micro particle loan, the financial application sector as represented by Tencent credit, covering multiple business forms such as fund wealth management, online credit, Internet banking lending, and Internet securities business.

1.Tenpay

Tenpay is a professional online payment platform officially launched by Tencent in September 2005, dedicated to providing secure, convenient and professional online payment services for Internet users and enterprises. Its core business is to help both parties performing transactions on the Internet to complete and receive payments. Tenpay services include user Tenpay account'recharge, cash withdrawal payment, and transaction management; and for corporate users, Tenpay also provides payment clearing services and auxiliary marketing services, wealth coupon services, lifestyle payment services, paipai shopping, film and television expo, air ticket ordering, game recharge, telephone recharge, lottery purchase and Tencent service purchase. In addition to the services listed above, Tenpay also provides merchant tools, with "Tenpay transaction buttons", "Website integration Tenpay", "Become a Tenpay merchant", and virtual goods intermediaries protection transactions and more functions as the main commodity tools.

2.We Chat Payment

Tencent We Chat Payment was officially launched with We Chat version 5.0 in August 2013, and external access applications were officially allowed in March 2014. We Chat payment is a payment function integrated on the We Chat client side, and users can complete the fast payment process through their mobile phones. We Chat payment is based on fast payment bound to bank cards and provides users with secure, fast and efficient payment services.

3.QQ Wallet

Tencent QQ Wallet is a mobile payment product that integrates a variety of convenient payment methods such as bank card payment, QR code payment, and NFC payment. QQ Wallet is committed to expanding the vertical scene business of young people, and has developed into an open platform that integrates multiple scenes and industries such as payment, living services, government services, financial management, and public welfare, providing users with comprehensive services covering clothing, food, shelter and transportation.

4.Licai Tong

Tencent Licai Tong works with financial institutions such as banks, insurance, funds, securities dealers, trusts and other companies to customize financial products that have fixed income, stocks and bonds and other fund types for users with different risk levels. Tencent Licai Tong has launched products such as salary fixed investment, dream plan, index fixed investment, credit card repayment and home loan wealth management to provide users with secure, stable, convenient, and diversified Internet wealth management services.

5.We Gold

WeGold is mainly used for asset security management. The gold share held by users in this service is registered and managed by ICBC. The service is only displayed and operated through the WeGold platform. Tenpay, as a third-party payment institution, fully protects the security of payment transaction funds and provides consulting services to users.

6.Tencent Great financial security

Tencent Great financial security is mainly a financial intelligent security prevention and control platform that provides security technology support and risk control solutions for Tencent Internet financial products such as We Chat Payment and QQ Wallet.

8.2.4.2 News from Tencent

In 2014, at the Global Partner Conference in Boao, Hainan, Tencent Credit Reporting surfaced; in 2015, licaitong achieved a scale of 100 billion yuan in capital; in 2016, Tencent's FiT business line and Tencent Cloud together promoted financial cloud. In addition to major financial technology companies such as Ant Financial, Lakala, JD Finance, and Tencent, China also has financial technology companies such as Xinhehui Wealth Management, Jinruilong, madailicai, China Tencent, Xiaohua Wallet and jingucaihang that try to provide a secure, convenient and stable Internet financial payment technology platform industry for enterprises, industry customers and investors .

8.3 Global creative insurance technology companies

The problems faced by the insurance market are: people think insurance is too complicated; its difficult for traditional companies to come up with overall solutions. Start-ups are trying to change the status quo of the insurance industry by combining insurance with social media to make insurance more concise and understandable, and better satisfy young peoples needs.

Here are 15 creative insurance technology companies:

1.Better View (US)

Better View is an insurance technology start-up that combines insurance and innovation engineering to capture aerial images through drones, identify potential problems with property targets, and submit reports to customers. This means that customers can clearly know which risks will have an adverse influence on their property and insure accordingly. Better View's business model is to collect personal data of each customer and provide personalized services for him.

2.Bought by Many (UK)

Bought by Many is also an insurtech start-up, covering pets, families, small items, and personal health. The company charges no fees and provides specific policies for traditional targets (French bulldogs). Bought by Many did not use the traditional insurance product assembly. Instead, it added a website to meet personal financing needs. At present, this website has more than 240,000 members, and the marketing method of Bought by Many may be effective.

3.Brolly (UK)

Brolly develops mobile apps based on artificial intelligence technology (AI) to provide consumers with free insurance management services. The company is committed to letting users quickly understand their needs, choose the insurance product that suits them, and save users time, money and energy. Brolly Advisor can analyze whether users are under-insured and what insurance is needed. Brolly Shop provides insurance products for consumers to choose from. Brolly Locker guarantees the security of users' policies.

4.Carpe Data (US)

Carpe Data provides risk assessment services for property and life insurance companies. The company extracts information from social media, the web, and wearable devices to predict the market performance of an insurance company's new product. Despite disputes over data protection in recent years, Carpe Data states that 85% of Internet users agree to share their information for the development of insurance products.

5.Cover (US)

Cover has launched an insurance pricing app. Take a picture of your personal belongings (jewelry, cars, houses, etc.) and transfer it to the app to get its underwriting price. At present, this app does not have insurance intermediary qualifications, and needs to rely on an insurance broker to match. Currently Cover has obtained insurance intermediary qualifications, and has established partnerships with more than 30 insurance companies throughout the United States. Users can download the software free of charge from Apple and Google App Stores, and through this software, they can consult relevant information about insurance products, and insure the right products according to personal circumstances .

6.Covi Analytics (UK)

CoVi Analytics tries to leverage data insights and automation programs to streamline compliance procedures and reduce compliance costs for insurance companies. At present, the UK insurance market has spent billions of pounds to prepare for paying. Through Covi Analytics, insurance companies can use software called "cmile" to operate better under decentralized supervision.

7.Give Surance (US)

As a financing platform, Give Surance works with certain insurance companies to encourage those who are enthusiastic about charity to insure them. The insurance company will return part of the premium paid by the policyholder to the personal credit account established by the policyholder at Give Surance, and donate it to the charity through the account.

8.Guevara (UK)

The Guevara network platform collects the user's auto insurance premiums to serve the purpose of saving premiums. Users can form a group with others on Guevara to gather some of the members' premiums together. If a member of the group has a low risk rate, all members of the group can save up to 50% of the premium.

9.Insurance A Thing (UK)

The aim of Insurance A Thing is to protect what you love say no to be obscure, refuse to talk rhetorically. The actual coverage of an insurance product is developed by a group of people who share the same idea and are generally recognized as impartial. Unlike traditional insurance companies, the insurance policy is easy to understand and there are no exclusion clauses, and the claims of the insured are processed quickly and lightning compensation is provided.

10.League (Canada)

League is a digital health platform for employers that can help companies better improve employee benefits. The platform integrates employees into the health benefits network system and provides diversified employee health products for employers to choose from, which not only brings convenience to employers, but also enables enterprises to save expenses. League intends to replace health insurance to become new digital health insurance, providing employees with the most valuable and convenient health products, enabling them to live a good life with employee benefits.

11.Lemonade (US)

Lemonade is a property insurance company. Users pay the company a small subscription fee each month to get the company's customized mobile insurance service. The company uses artificial intelligence robots to complete underwriting in just 90 seconds. This service is available on OS, Android and desktop computers. Currently, the company only serves in New York, but it plans to expand its operations across the UK. The company received $ 13 million of investment in 2015.

12.Simply Business (UK)

Simply Business is the UK's largest online insurance company. The company initially offered online comparison services for insurance products for SMEs, including policies from Ava, Hiscox, QBE and Zurich. To keep up with the pace of digital finance, the company began tailoring insurance products that customers can quickly apply.

13.So-sure (UK)

So-sure is a mobile phone insurance company that allows users and their friends to connect accounts and get cash back every year. So-sure means "Social Insurance", a new concept of insurance that is truly reassuring. As long as the users phone is not lost or damaged (ie no claim), they can connect accounts with friends and get up to 80% cash back every year. So-sure sets up Reward Pots for each user. At the end of each year, when no claims are made by users and friends, cash can be withdrawn from the reward pots.

14.Spixii.ai (UK)

Spixii.ai conducts underwriting business using artificial intelligence and machine learning technologies. The start-up haves intelligent insurance agents (also known as chatbots) talk to customers, providing customers with convenient and fast personalized services.

15.Trov (UK)

Trov is an insurance technology company that aims to transform insurance in the mobile era, offering new options to customers who are unwilling to insure because of complex policies. Through the Trov application, users can access the insurance platform, which will provide real-time pricing for different insurable standards, according to user needs.